CRAZY
MAKERS

Getting Along with the
Difficult People in Your Life

PAUL MEIER, M.D.
ROBERT L. WISE, PH.D.

THOMAS NELSON PUBLISHERS®
Nashville

A Division of Thomas Nelson, Inc.
www.ThomasNelson.com

Published in Nashville, Tennessee, by Thomas Nelson, Inc.

Personal names and details of personal stories have been changed to protect identities.

All Scripture quotations are from THE NEW KING JAMES VERSION unless otherwise designated. Copyright © 1982 by Thomas Nelson, Inc. Used by permission. All rights reserved.

Scriptures marked KJV are from the King James Version of the Bible.

Scripture quotations marked NIV are taken from *THE HOLY BIBLE, NEW INTERNATIONAL VERSION. NIV.* Copyright © 1973, 1978, 1984 by International Bible Society. Used by permission of Zondervan Publishing House. All rights reserved.

Scripture quotations marked NASB are taken from the NEW AMERICAN STANDARD BIBLE ®, Copyright © The Lockman Foundation 1960, 1962, 1963, 1968, 1971, 1972, 1973, 1975, 1977. Used by permission.

Library of Congress Cataloging-in-Publication Data

Meier, Paul D.
    Crazymakers : getting along with the difficult people in your life /
Paul Meier, Robert L. Wise.
        p. cm.
    ISBN 0-7852-7870-2 (hardcover)
    1. Conflict management—Religious aspects—Christianity. I. Wise,
Robert L. II. Title.
BV4597.53.C58M45 2003
158.2—dc22   2003020494

Printed in the United States of America

1 2 3 4 5 6 — 07 06 05 04 03

Contents

PART ONE

Crazymaking Everywhere!

PART TWO
Getting the "Crazy" Out:
Six Steps out of Your Crisis

PART THREE
Beyond Crazy:
The Gift of Spiritual Endurance

part**ONE**

CRAZYMAKING
EVERYWHERE!

Living with insensitive, tactless, careless,

inattentive, difficult, self-absorbed,

neglectful, damaging, condemning, harsh,

hard, treacherous, deceiving, prejudiced,

and paralyzing people

chapter ONE

Meet the Enemy

This book is personal, very personal.

If you've ever felt caught between the wall and a human pile driver, beating you into emotional oblivion, you have learned how personal an emotional attack can be. In addition to the embarrassment and confusion, you also discovered how those crazy moments leave you wrung out and perplexed.

One of the most painful surprises in the aftermath is the discovery that someone you thought was your friend was actually a battering ram. Often we don't develop this insight until the conflict is over and we've been hurt by someone we care about, someone we thought cared about us. When the adversary turns out to be a colleague, supervisor, friend, or—most difficult—your spouse, you will need help and insight to know how to handle the complex issues staring you in the face.

In the last decade our entire society has taken a hard look at physical abuse. New laws have been enacted, and the word has gone out that we won't tolerate people getting hurt bodily. Now the time is approaching when we must look more firmly at verbal abuse. What can you do about a person who attacks you with barbed words? You're familiar with the childhood retort, "Sticks and stones may break my bones, but names will never hurt me." But the truth is that names—and other hurtful words—can break our hearts and inflict pain to our most precious feelings. Our adversaries seem to have a unique ability to find the exact words that cut to the bone and leave us bleeding in the street.

In the following pages we are going to help you find new ways to confront and handle the difficult people who consistently drive you toward the edge of sanity. We will offer new possibilities for handling difficult situations. And we'll give examples of people who have struggled with difficult people. Let's start with Jack.

Jack Smith was the beloved, successful pastor of a church in Dallas, Texas, but his problems at home reduced him to wanting to hide under a rock. When the arguments with his wife heated up, he could feel the anger bubbling up in his throat, but he couldn't turn the emotion into constructive action. Jack had ridden down the same hard, bumpy road with his wife a hundred times, and every trip was always the same. No matter what the problem, Ann started shouting, and then her voice escalated into screaming. Jack inevitably ended up backtracking, and their problems never got solved. Their current argument was no different.

"I've *told you* a million times to lock the door when you go to work. Do you realize how difficult it is to live with you?" Ann's eyes narrowed and became increasingly hard. "You have the brain power of a bird. Why can't you simply *listen to me*?"

Jack took a deep breath. "Last night we discussed the plan that I would leave the back door unlocked when I left this morning so you wouldn't have to worry about finding a key when you came back from jogging." He bit the side of his mouth and paused for a moment. "The trouble is you forgot to set the lock after you returned. Then you went to work and left the house open all day." Jack threw up his hands. "Look. Let's not make a mountain out of a molehill. Everyone makes mistakes. Let's simply agree about what we will do from now on."

"You idiot!" Ann hissed. "You *always* blame *your* mistakes on me! I'm always the one to discredit. There's no point in even talking to you." She started poking at him with her index finger, jabbing like a sword. "You won't accept any responsibility for your mistakes. Well, I'm not going to take it any longer!"

"Look, Ann. I left the back door unlocked for you. My

concern is leaving the house open all day when someone could walk in and steal our stuff. You're flying off the handle because I mentioned a mistake you made."

"*I* made? You're the one who's responsible for locking the house," Ann charged as her face flushed pink and her lower lip trembled. "All you do is push me." Ann slammed a book on the table so hard the lamp shook.

The pastor's anger turned into fear of what Ann might do next. A number of times she had broken furniture and occasionally slapped him. By this point in their marriage, she could shift from being piqued to uncontrollable in a flash. Jack hated these violent confrontations; he knew they had to stop, but he had no idea how to reverse the uproar. The best Jack could do was attempt to walk softly around Ann.

"Ann," Jack said firmly, "you are upset because the house was left unlocked all day; but nothing happened. No one stole anything. The trouble is, we can't even talk about an issue without a storm erupting. That's why I'm asking you to go to counseling with me."

"*You worm!*" Ann shrieked. "You're always looking for somebody who will join your side of the fight. You've probably got some old buddy-buddy, religious counselor in your hip pocket." Doubling her fist and shaking it in Jack's face, Ann blasted away. "Go by yourself, jerk! You're the one who needs help."

"Come on, Ann. The problem is that a door was left unlocked."

"No," Ann insisted, "the problem is you're a spiritually insensitive person. You have the religious commitment of a heathen. When I listen to you rail at me, I'm not even sure you are a Christian." She stormed out of the room and turned the corner to go upstairs.

Jack heard Ann stomping up to their bedroom. He looked down and discovered his hands shaking slightly. Once again a simple problem of miscommunication had erupted into a world war. Jack kept thinking that if he could explain issues better to Ann, their problems could be fixed before people at the church knew about them.

Jack had always been good at working with the people in his church and had helped many people with their marital problems. Why couldn't he do any better at home? he wondered.

It took Jack quite a while to realize that his wife was a crazymaker.

Confronting the Problem

As the cartoon character Pogo once said, "We have met the enemy and he is us." Difficult people often seem to have an uncanny ability to make us feel like we are the source of the problems. By the time we have finished trying to make some sense out of the argument, we feel like the plug on our mental machine has been flipped off, and we are reduced to gibbering idiots.

Are we? *No.*

Psychiatrist Paul Meier and Pastor Robert L. Wise are constantly counseling with people whose personal struggles with difficult people have made them feel disturbed, disregarded, and disoriented because the other person did an "end run" on the conversation and turned them upside down. When the enemy is a spouse, a child, an employer, or a fellow employee, unavoidable closeness causes particular trouble. Those who know us best have the intimacy levels to allow their knowing our weaknesses. They know which words will confuse us or simply shut us down. It can feel like a no-win situation, as though our opponent is using subversive or diverting techniques so that we can neither understand nor be understood. Confusion abounds *constantly.*

We need help in understanding our crazymakers!

Unraveling the Ball of Yarn

We have created the word *crazymaker* to describe these difficult people. Our best attempts at talking to difficult people turn into torment because they aren't actually interested in communicating. Their goal is to dominate the exchange in such a manner that they will come out of the conversation looking better than they went in. The way they "feel" is more important to them than harmony with us. When we are dealing with such manipulation, the result is that we inevitably feel unhooked from our true selves.

We define crazymakers as . . .

People who consistently irritate and confront without taking responsibility or recognizing their own limitations. They do not feel the impact or hurt caused by their constant and incessant obstinate behavior. Crazymaker behavior ranges from being argumentative to being destructive. Depending on their lack of empathy, crazymakers move by degrees from being difficult to being narcissistic. Totally self-absorbed, narcissistic persons are marked by indifference and unconcern.

Most people have not stopped to consider how crazymakers think and operate. We assume people are simply "folks." When something goes wrong, we assume it must be our fault, and as a result, we often don't analyze why these conversations and encounters turn out to be so disastrous. *And that's our problem.* We need help in learning how to understand crazymakers.

Jack Smith was a seminary graduate and naturally adept at working with people. Members of his congregation loved

Jack and believed him to be a sensitive person. His wife, Ann, could also be quite charming and gave church members every reason to believe she adored them. Usually when something irritated her, Ann left the church through the back door and no one saw her explode. The Smiths' problem stayed wellhidden behind their living-room curtains.

When Jack finally turned to a professional counselor, he discovered that Ann was a crazymaker, which was his first step in learning to understand why Ann was so indifferent.

Recognizing a Crazymaker

In our practices we see two different types of crazymakers: difficult people and narcissistic, self-absorbed persons. The difference between these two crazymakers is a decreasing amount of emotional involvement, which translates into an increasing amount of pain-inflicting behavior. Any argument can turn into a full-scale calamity when one or both of the parties have no concern for other people. A lack of affection ultimately produces the destructive behavior of a narcissist.

THE DIFFICULT PERSON

These crazymakers have indifferent feelings for others, which leads them to make destructive responses to others.

These crazymakers are the insensitive, tactless, careless, and inattentive people you sometimes encounter. However, many difficult people still have a degree of empathy for others. They are a mixture of kindness and selfishness that often confuses us.

THE NARCISSISTIC, SELF-ABSORBED PERSON

These crazymakers have absolutely *no* concern for others, which leads them to make treacherous or manipulative, attacking responses to others. Narcissists are the self-absorbed, neglectful, damaging, condemning, harsh, hard, treacherous, deceiving, prejudiced, and paralyzing people you sometimes encounter. They are only kind to people who make them feel important or whom they can manipulate. Their kindness, unlike the difficult person's occasional genuine kindness, lacks empathy and sincere compassion.

The Point?

If your encounters with a particular person tend to leave you feeling crazy, it is quite possible that this individual may not have significant feelings for other human beings and will easily turn into a treacherous adversary. In effect, narcissistic crazymakers are "emotionally challenged," and they don't realize how serious their problem is. They may seem "warm" some of the time, but the truth is their hearts are actually icebergs.

Look again at the narcissistic person. If this crazymaker has lost all empathy, you can bet that his or her reactions will be highly destructive to you and other people.

What's Ahead?

In the following chapters we will help you recognize how the problem of being "emotionally challenged" causes the difficult people in your world to treat you with such callous insensitivity. While the difference between a narcissist and a difficult person may not seem great when you are looking at it on a piece of paper, you will discover that if these two came walking through your front door in the flesh and detonated in your living room, the gulf between them is enormous! Probably many people reading this book could immediately stand up and shout, "Yes! Now I understand! I am dealing with a narcissist!"

Anyone who has lived with the impossible reactions and demands of a truly narcissistic crazymaker can testify to how deep and enduring the struggle has been. These strugglers have often lost faith in their relationships' future because they do not see any alternative to what they have experienced in the past.

Yet this book offers hope! The following chapters will take you inside the world of crazymakers and help you understand how to deal with them. As we follow Jack and Ann Smith and other people as they face these problems, you will gain insight into how crazymakers think. The effect that difficult people have on children and the church will be explored. And help will be offered for facing the problems at the office.

In addition, you will be given six steps to help you walk out of the crisis you are now facing. And you will discover how the Christian faith offers concrete help in turning these struggles into successes.

Don't give up. A better day is ahead!

chapterTWO

The Battle Begins

For eleven months, Jack went once a week to one of the Meier Clinics, where the therapist listened carefully as the pastor poured out his woes. Jack found that this opportunity to unburden his heart gave him the confidence to continue in his troubled marriage. Ann not only didn't go with him, but she resisted any conversation about what he was learning.

"Look," Ann said emphatically one evening, "I'm glad you're getting some help out of the talks, but don't try to pressure me. I don't even want to hear any more about this."

Ann's cold response ended the discussion, and Jack knew that his attempting to resurrect the topic would turn another disagreement into a disaster. His time with the counselor would have to be only his own time. Yet Jack still did not know who would be coming through his living-room door on any given night.

On some evenings Ann arrived home as a happy, carefree wife. Supper would be delightful and the evening pure pleasure. On other evenings, the bride of Dracula swept in ready for another kill. Ann would be irate over some meaningless issue that had hit her wrong. Any attempt at resolution ended in turbulence, leaving everyone hanging over the edge.

Over a period of time, Ann had spent a great deal of money behind Jack's back. When he found out exactly how much his wife had squandered, Jack nearly had a heart attack. In an irresponsible and unaccountable way, Ann had bought over eight thousand dollars worth of odds and ends for no other reason except the premise she "deserved it." Jack could see no way to work them out of such a deep and unexpected debt. After a considerable discussion, they decided on a method to erase Ann's debt. She wanted to sell Tupperware and was convinced her profit would pay back the deficit.

"Look," Jack said firmly, "I'm not going to put any extra money into this venture. You must put a significant amount of money back in a savings account each month to cover the cost of resupplying your inventory as well as paying back the money you spent. The entire reason is for *you* to repay the debt you owe."

Ann bit her lip. "Okay. Okay," she answered. "I'll put the money back. Don't worry."

Jack nodded. "I'll be expecting a significant return by the end of the year."

Twelve months later Jack sat down with Ann to examine how the year had gone. Jack extended his hand. "Where are your books?"

"You know I'm not good at bookkeeping."

"I understand. Let me see the books."

Ann looked guilty. "I'm sorry. I guess I really didn't keep them very well. As a matter of fact, I didn't write much of anything down on paper."

Jack's mouth dropped. "You've got to be kidding!"

"I'm sorry. I'm sorry." Ann had a hint of irritation in her voice. "I know I should have done it, but I didn't. There's no point in arguing about an innocent mistake."

Jack ran his hands nervously through his hair, trying not to explode. He took a deep breath and pressed on. "Where's the money you were supposed to deposit in a savings account to buy new inventory?"

"I guess that didn't work out either." Ann smiled innocently. "Sometimes we get interruptions in our life."

"Interruptions!" Jack wanted to throttle his wife. "What did you do with the extra money that came in from the profits?"

Ann looked blank. "I don't know."

Jack fell back in his chair and rolled his eyes. "I simply can't believe that you have nothing to show for correcting a problem that was completely and entirely yours in the first place."

"Let's not dwell on the past," Ann said. "The important thing is for us to go forward."

"Forward!" Jack clenched his fist. "And how are you going *to do that?*"

"Just loan me two hundred dollars, and this time I'll make everything work out right."

"I told you I wouldn't give you any extra money!"

"Jack," Ann's tone of irritation stayed in her voice, "do you want me to fix this problem or not? I can't do it without some more money."

Jack almost felt dizzy. "How in the world did we ever get into such a mess?"

"Two hundred dollars will cover the error." Ann remained resolute.

After a considerable amount of discussion, Jack yielded out of fear that the problem would spin further out of control. He insisted that Ann promise to spend no more than two hundred dollars. She agreed, and Jack hoped the problem was over. Was it?

Sixty days later the inventory bills came in. Ann had spent three hundred dollars and was indifferent about the error. Jack was almost beside himself. "Do you realize what you have done?" he pushed.

"Look! Don't get uppity with me, Jack. You've lost a job before and were out of work. This problem isn't any different. Good heavens! You act like you have no idea of what it's like to struggle with unemployment."

"Unemployment?" Jack raised his eyebrows. "What's unemployment got to do with any of this?"

"The issue is your blaming me for a lack of money."

"Lack of money?"

"You know what the truth is? I can't trust you financially!" Ann crossed her arms resolutely over her chest. "The real issue here is the way you have no integrity with money. You leave me little choice but to struggle on by myself."

"Ann," Jack begged. "Get serious!"

"Serious?" Ann's eyes flashed. "Here I am doing everything I can to straighten out this mess and all I get from you is criticism and bad-mouthing. Nag, nag, nag. Jack, do you realize that's all you do?"

Jack gawked in amazement, unsure of what to say next. His first impulse was to feel that he was stingy and selfish. Maybe she was right. But Jack didn't buckle to his feelings because he knew Ann had created the turmoil to avoid facing her irresponsible actions. The business project began as an attempt to eradicate a debt, as well as to cover business expenses, not spend more money. What made the matter feel so crazy to Jack was that Ann really believed her own accusations.

Sorting Out the Mess

Approximately a year after beginning counseling, Jack Smith returned to the counselor's office to discuss another recurring situation wherein Ann flew off the handle and accused Jack of incompetence. After talking for half an hour, the counselor leaned forward and said, "Jack, you are not facing reality."

Jack blinked several times. "I . . . I . . . don't think I understand."

"You believe her accusation," the counselor said.

"Well," Jack paused and thought for a moment. "Sure. I believe what Ann says."

"That's the problem! It's why we aren't making any progress."

Jack shook his head. "I don't think I get what you're saying."

"You think *you're the problem*," the counselor insisted. "You've got to stop believing all the nonsense this woman is putting on you. Certainly you have issues, but that's not what's wrong with your marriage." The counselor looked Jack straight in the eye. "The problem isn't you. *It's her!* But *you* can take responsibility for learning how to protect yourself from *her*."

Jack was speechless. For virtually an entire year, he had assumed that he was a good part of the problems in their marriage.

Recognizing the Adversary

Crazymakers generally hit us with such boldness and seeming self-assurance that we naturally believe they must be competent. While we don't believe we are wrong on the issues under discussion, our tendency is to assume difficult people are naturally "one-up" on us. The time has come to take off all the masks and discover whom the opponent actually is!

Behind the fierce head butting, crazymakers often have a contradictory set of issues that we wouldn't expect. Like a football team racing from goal post to goal post, self-absorbed people are caught between two poles. On one end is grandiosity; at the other is worthlessness. Difficult people are generally chasing back and forth between a level of esteem that is either too high or too low. Many times their arduous confrontations are actually attempts to cover up moments when someone has just scored at the goal post of their low self-esteem.

Weakness, not power, is at the bottom of their aggression.

But your recognizing the heart of *their problem* does not change anything. If you suddenly confronted them with their neediness, you would probably get whacked in the mouth. They are running from this secret of their inadequacy as hard as they can. It is the last truth they want to hear.

Ann Smith's resistance to counseling is typical. She couldn't allow herself to recognize the pain of her own limitations.

And it's easy for crazymakers to hide their problems from themselves and others because they are socially skilled people who are initially quite likable. People often don't see difficult people in anything but a positive light until they come very close to the person.

But once these difficult people are cornered or pushed, their negative side erupts. Friendly, hospitable crazymakers are capable of anger, hostility, manipulation, and devastating attacks.

That's where the battle begins!

An Increasing Problem

The growing number of divorces and the resulting breakdown of American family life have enormously increased the problem of crazymaking. The percentage of American teenagers who are suicidal or addicted has risen 300 percent in the past fifty years due to this breakup, which also produces children who assume family problems are their fault. Often the loss of one of the parents creates in a child an abnormal need to be loved, which can lead the child toward narcissism. This disruption at home produces a disruption in the child. As the divorce statistics rise, the crazymakers increase. Fifty years ago, the average citizen wouldn't have much idea what crazymaking was. Today, the problem is rampant in every community in America.

Ordinary People is an excellent book and movie that depicts how a narcissistic mother affects everyone around her. The woman's self-absorption ruins the most important relationships in her life, and she is unable to see it! The tragedy of crazymakers is that their being "emotionally challenged" prevents them from grasping their own serious problem.

Because this problem is on the increase, you must remember several facts that will help you keep a confrontation in perspective. You might want to put these insights on a card and carry it with you, reminding you of the truth when you are confronted by a difficult person. Then you can reorder your own thinking so you can find the right approach when the battle starts.

FACTS TO REMEMBER

1. The problem arises from the crazymaker's weakness, not his or her strength. It helps to remember the person's pain is what keeps him or her from responding properly.

2. In addition to low self-esteem, crazymakers struggle with pent-up anger. They often explode for reasons that have nothing to do with the confrontation at hand.

3. Crazymakers are growing in number. Don't be surprised when you encounter one.

Identifying the Battlefield

The following test is based on a narcissism assessment developed by Peter Kuiper, President of Christian Counseling Ministries. It is designed to help identify crazy-makers with the needs discussed above. Take this opportunity to see how the person you are struggling with stands up to this measuring stick.

CRAZYMAKER QUESTIONNAIRE

Think about the person you are struggling with and check the statements that apply to him or her.

IMAGE-KEEPING

This person . . .

○ always promotes his or her own self-image.

○ uses people as extensions of himself or herself.

○ does not seem to sense that he or she should be more tactful.

○ is willing to distort reality to maintain his or her own fantasies about who he or she is.

○ treats disagreement or disobedience as disloyalty.

○ responds with vengefulness or vindictiveness when he or she thinks you are being disloyal.

○ sees himself or herself as special or unique.

○ is willing to be destructive in order to be seen in a light of his or her own choosing.

○ is deeply bothered if his or her image is diminished by other people.

ENTITLEMENT

This person . . .

○ expects special treatment.

○ thrives on the adoration and admiration of others and will seek it out regardless of the cost.

○ rolls over people without noticing that he or she may be stepping on another person's toes.

○ often feels that the world owes him or her glory or respect.

○ seeks out people who don't know him or her personally to maintain this adoration and feeling of self-importance.

○ seems to be insensitive to how he or she affects others.

○ does not appear to care about others.

EXPLOITATION

This person . . .

○ is manipulative and controlling.

○ often abuses his or her position of influence and power while maintaining that this is for the other person's good.

○ alternates between the extremes of idealizing himself or herself and devaluing himself or herself.

○ sometimes exaggerates your positive characteristics or ideals.

○ sometimes makes a radical change from caring about someone to being completely indifferent to this person.

○ will resort to put-downs or highly critical judgments.

○ becomes somewhat paranoid or may see opposition as part of a conspiracy.

○ seems to think he or she has a right to ignore others.

○ rarely admits personal failure and is adept at blame-shifting.

○ does not care how his or her behavior affects others.

○ uses other people's weaknesses to maintain a power position.

○ has no hesitation or shame in conning others.

○ isn't bothered when he or she makes people uncomfortable.

O develops relationships that tend to be superficial and shallow.

O makes you feel off-balance or "crazy" at times.

DEPERSONALIZATION

This person . . .

O lacks genuine empathy.

O does not seem to have significant feelings for others.

O will not compromise or negotiate fairly.

O sometimes treats other people like things or objects.

O has used denial, arrogance, haughtiness, charm, and exaggeration or persuasion to maintain a "superior" position.

O is good at convincing you of his or her goodness—and of your badness.

O expects automatic compliance with his or her expectations.

O seems to retreat from genuine human need and ignores the pain of others.

O sees solutions and success as more important than personal relationships.

O does not seem to feel the struggle when others are involved in personal pain.

If you checked twenty to thirty-five of these questions, your crazymaker is definitely a *difficult person*. Beyond that score you are probably dealing with a *narcissist*.

Think it over. You need to pay attention to the crazymakers in your world . . . before they pay attention to you!

chapter THREE

Life in an Emotional
Straightjacket

Fortunately, when we see our problems from a different angle, our understanding changes: *Insight helps change our perspective.* As we perceive the problem in greater depth, we are able to see aspects that were formerly camouflaged. The answers were waiting there to be discovered, but we missed them.

After hours of counseling, Reverend Jack Smith saw his domestic wars in a much clearer light. He began to see that his wife was neither an insensitive nor a difficult person. He worried that she might, in fact, be narcissistic. Certainly Ann operated very differently than he originally thought. In the first years of the marriage, Jack didn't have a clue that

Ann's entire approach to every argument was concealed in her hidden agenda. Of course, even Ann wasn't aware of her own intentions.

As we talk about the unseen objectives of difficult people, we need to be aware these individuals have lost sight of the pain that long ago settled over the center of their own lives. Their actions, arguments, and responses seem rational and quite plausible to them. Their attacks seem logical and natural to them. They push you to the edge of your own stability by proclaiming what they believe is true . . . when it isn't!

One evening the Smiths argued for twenty minutes without getting anywhere. Jack could tell the disagreement was heating up, but he wasn't about to stop because he believed he could demonstrate that his position was correct.

"I'm sorry," Ann abruptly said in the heat of the disagreement. "I honestly don't agree with you, but I know I've overreacted." Tears formed in the corner of her eyes. "I didn't mean to get so cross, but sometimes I simply seem to explode. Please forgive me, Jack."

Jack's mouth dropped slightly. He knew Ann was totally wrong in pushing him to clean the garage; he had rearranged the tools and swept the floor only a week earlier. Ann generally parked her car in the driveway so she probably hadn't even looked inside the garage. But seldom did Jack hear an apology! He was caught completely off guard. "Of course!"

He held out his arms to hug Ann. "I'm always glad to forgive you." Ann smiled and said nothing more.

Life in the Smith house returned to normal and Jack felt relieved. His new approach to their problems was making a difference because Ann was now apologetic. Maybe something he had learned in one of his counseling sessions was rubbing off on her.

Two hours later while Jack was getting ready to go to bed, Ann stuck her head out of the bathroom. "Jack," she said with an edge in her voice, "we *do need* to get your tools off your workbench."

Jack froze in place. All the tools were already on the wall, but Ann still didn't realize it. *Nothing had changed.* She had a strong need to control Jack and fight with him in order to release some of her lifelong venom. Her mom had been totally unpredictable—seemingly sweet at times but explosive with verbal and sometimes even physical abuse toward Ann at other times. Ann's father was passive and feared Ann's rejection, spoiling her rotten, which resulted in Ann's getting constantly angry at others in the world who didn't reinforce the entitlement she learned from her father. She was almost like a substitute wife to him. He adored Ann because he had no relationship with Ann's mother; he avoided her as much as possible. Ann's concerns about the tools in the garage were nothing more than a power play to keep her husband in the place she always had kept her father: submission. Feeling like iron bands were being tightened around his head, he didn't answer, but stared blankly at the nightstand in front of him. Ann's apology had only been a maneuver!

Crazy Strategies!

Most people do not conduct conversations in combative ways. What comes out of their mouths is essentially what they feel in their hearts. Not so with a difficult person! If you are encountering a narcissistic person, the problems become even more difficult to handle.

Self-absorbed people generally maintain clandestine plans, because they desire to conceal their weaknesses. On top of this their diminished sense of empathy keeps them from "feeling" how this duplicity affects other people. Rather than being *relationally oriented*, they are *agenda driven*. You probably want to have friends who care about you and will talk about whatever is on your heart. Not these people! They are focused on their own inner agenda, which they learned in early childhood in most cases.

The result? Crazy strategies abound!

Ann's apology was a maneuver to get her out of the doghouse when she was losing the argument. Her diminished feelings for Jack produced their *confrontations*. When difficult people lose the battle, they respond with *clever manipulations*. Sound dark? Perhaps not. These people may not even recognize their own attempts at control. Our purpose is not to demonize difficult people, but to help you develop insight into how they function. You need to stand back and recognize what is happening behind the scene.

Go back to the corollary this chapter began with: *Insight helps change our perspective*. Reversing this corollary is also part of the answer: *Changing our perspective gives us insight!* If we climb to a higher vantage point, beyond the heated exchanges, we can fully understand why difficult people perform as they do.

Dr. Robert Wise has a home at 8,500 feet in Colorado, near the valley where he grew up as a boy. An avid mountain climber, he loves to wander through the forests, trying to make sense out of how the valleys tie together. Recently a pilot friend offered to fly him over these peaks as well as around the mountains in the area. Robert had always been intrigued about what was on the other side of those peaks and looked forward to the flight in a small one-engine airplane.

As they zoomed over the top of the peaks, Robert was able to look down and see not only the valley, but also the whole mountain range for the first time in his life. He could now understand how the deep winding valleys and the meandering mountains fit together. Looking down on familiar terrain made a world of difference in what he saw. *Changing his perspective gave him insight!*

Jack Smith's counseling experience helped develop personal insight, correcting his lack of perspective on what was happening in their family quarrels. If we are going to learn how to work with self-absorbed people, we must have both long-range perspective and personal, close-up insight.

Where in the World Do They Come From?

Jack could now emotionally perch on the ceiling and look down on the "clean-up-the-garage" fight. He also learned some important data about why people like Ann can be so obstinate. They didn't happen to be difficult by accident! A large variety of factors can contribute to the development of narcissism in a child.

Self-absorbed individuals have problems that go back to somewhere between fifteen and twenty-four months of age. At that time these children received emotional injuries that damaged their emotional development. Here are three of the most common parenting practices that produce narcissists.

1. *Spoil the child.* Everyone is born with naturally narcissistic tendencies. There's nothing wrong with that proclivity. It's only human. We said "no" before we learned to say "yes." When we didn't get what we wanted, we immedi-

ately screamed with a murderous rage. If another toddler tried to grab one of our toys, we were ready to commit a felony to stop the intrusion. The one word we understood very well was always *"MINE!"*

If you ask a cranky two-year-old if he wants to breathe today, he is quite likely to yell "No!" or simply be defiant. This behavior is not abnormal and maintains an important part of the child's development called *individuation*. A child needs to become separate from his mother and learn to think for himself, so individualization is necessary and even healthy if the child still learns limits and doesn't grow up thinking the world revolves around him and that he or she is always en- titled to be in control. Ann's father always gave in to Ann at all her growth stages, producing her narcissistic attitudes.

However, some of the obstinacy is plain old inborn self- ishness. If his parents give in to the consequences of his self- ish behavior, the child will assume such nastiness is normal and acceptable.

On the other hand, discipline teaches us to be afraid of our selfishness and our parents' disapproval. We begin to develop a conscience and become more civilized. When love is added by both word and deeds, we are on our way to turn- ing into wonderful adults who have outgrown most (but never all) of our narcissism. The problems come when we have been spoiled and don't learn to give up these behaviors! Difficult behavior is waiting in the wings!

2. Abuse the child. Tragically, many adults were badly treated when they were small children. Nevertheless, many of these individuals grow up to become considerate, loving people. However, when children are constantly abused verbally, physically, and certainly sexually, they usually grow up to harbor anger and hostility at the authority figures in their world. As they act out their negative feelings, explosive situations develop, increasing their problems. Then these people tend to become even more selfish, defiant, and hostile. The possibility of their not surviving is an issue that hides in the back of their minds.

In extreme instances, abuse can lead to highly destructive behavior. Many times the more severely injured individuals turn into dangerous psychopaths who exchange their anger for another's pain. Psychiatrists working in prisons have discovered a disproportionate number of inmates were abused as children.

Parents must understand how important it is to love their children. Abuse is always a dead-end street! Ann's mother had been verbally and physically abusive with Ann, and an unpredictable caregiver.

3. Inconsistent mothering. How any child is cared for has serious consequences for the future, either for the best or the worst. If newborn babies aren't held when lonely or clothed when cold, they begin to develop a destructive image of their mother. Without the capacity to think or reflect, these children start to develop a "bad mother" idea about their parent. In turn, they also form a "bad child" image of themselves. Lack of attention that eats into these children's self-concepts starts to devour positive self-esteem. They have started down a hard road. The more neglected a baby or infant is the more narcissistic, hostile, and controlling he or she tends to become. Ann's mother seldom met her needs, yelled at Ann, and even hit her. Ann learned "don't exist" messages (nonverbally) from her mother's reactions.

For reasons that are not yet completely understood, children who are brought up in mayhem often develop into what is clinically called "borderline personality," which is a dysfunctional type of narcissism. When they become adults, these persons are hostile and often force people to "walk on eggshells" around them, to avoid tripping a reaction that can ignite anger.

The more "out of control" a child feels in infancy, the more controlling he becomes to compensate and self-protect. These people tend to be black-and-white thinkers who don't tolerate ambiguity well. They tend to see the people around them as being either all good or all bad. Gray doesn't seem to have much of a place in their vocabulary. These borderline personalities will idolize you and then in the next instant write you off as hopeless. When you switch from the top seat to the bottom of the ladder, you also discover the anger they are waiting to fire at someone. Watch out! They can give new meaning to crazymaking.

The movie *Fatal Attraction* depicted how dangerous a borderline person can be. In the movie, the viewer watches the borderline personality jump from one overly dependent relationship to another as she becomes increasingly destructive. Every therapist has seen these persons move on from one therapist to the next, seeking a more satisfying (but false) answer to their problems. If the clinician doesn't do what they want, these individuals abruptly start hating him or her and are ready to go on to another counselor. They will keep running until they find a professional who is afraid to cross them or only cares about money and therefore gives in to their inordinate demands. Their issue isn't change; they want to be placated.

While an outsider might observe these families and see normal children being cared for by normal parents in a normal way, the children cease to believe they are "normal." The parents push an "image" of how they want their children to be by projecting a sense of the child's being special. The little ones begin to consider themselves in grandiose terms. The children's genuine self-image is quickly lost as they try to achieve the parents' image. Their task is to live up to the parents' goals, not to their own ideals. Of course, these children cannot achieve this task, and feelings of worthlessness soon slide into the picture. Such internal pressures force them to strive after power and control, developing the tendency to be seductive and manipulative. Their inner agenda is now focused on issues of power and control.

When children mature without this problem being addressed, the groundwork has been laid for the same difficulties to be perpetuated in the next generation. Injured parents expect their children to provide them the understanding they did not receive. Injured people injure people! And they look toward their children to mirror the image of themselves that they need in order to consider themselves adequate. This can come in a verbal affirmation, a smile, or a gesture of affirmation. For example, a mother who is obsessed with her appearance may often ask one of her children, "How do I look?" However, she is not seeking an objective answer. The woman wants the child to respond, "Mother, you look wonderful!" At that point the child has become a mirror.

Of course, the child can't perform this task, but the parent's needs are still impressed on his or her psyche. The issues continue on and on.

Rather than sharing feeling and emotion with other people, the tendency of narcissists is to dominate others, regardless of the pain they cause. Now Jack Smith recognized this dimension in his wife's behavior. He began to operate with a new sense of perspective that told him his wife's problems started a long time before they met.

Look at the Bible

Remember the story of King Saul in the Old Testament? A very significant person, Saul led the transition from Israel's days as a nation made up of independent tribes to Israel's becoming a kingdom. He was a strong young man, taller by head and shoulders than any of the rest of the soldiers. And he was a devout Jewish believer who loved God. Saul was quickly recognized as a great warrior and became king.

However, when young David appeared on the scene, a different sort of man started to emerge in Saul. Even though David was a faithful follower of King Saul, David soon encountered a suspicious, crafty, treacherous monarch who was out to destroy him. Defining Saul as a difficult person is truly an understatement! This unpredictable, frightened king of Israel turned into a tyrant of monstrous proportions. His almost never-ending attempts to kill David provide some of the most interesting reading in the Bible. It doesn't take long to recognize that you are reading about a very dangerous crazymaker.

David's response to Saul offers a three-step process for us to follow today.

Step 1: Remember that you aren't the issue! David knew the problem was with Saul, not with himself. Jack Smith also achieved an important perspective. He recognized that the source of conflicts with Ann lay in her emotional makeup. Ann's maneuvers didn't obscure his view. He might periodically still feel confused, but now Jack knew he wasn't the issue.

Step 2: Recognize you can't cure the other person. David couldn't straighten Saul out and Jack Smith couldn't "fix" Ann! Yet if you care about difficult people, you naturally want to help them get their lives in order. Everything in you will yearn to reassemble the broken parts and make their emotional machines run right.

Sorry. You can't! If you want to have peace of mind, you must realize you cannot change a crazymaker's internal workings. Often victims of these people engage in endless forays to enter the minds of narcissists in order to tinker with their mental machinery and make a different set of responses happen. Again, sorry. Change is possible only because each one of us has decided to change ourselves. No one can do it for us. Insanity is often described as "doing the same things over and over again and expecting different results." Jack had tried the same old attempts to fix Ann and had gotten nothing but pain as a result.

Step 3: We can only change ourselves. Instead of responding to Saul in a like manner, David refused to become Saul's enemy.

David supported the king even as he hid from Saul's vicious attacks. Jack Smith also made a decision to change his own attitude; he would not accept Ann's harsh and generally unjustified criticisms. If she made an accusation, he would dismiss it if he knew it was unfounded. This third step alone kept Jack from living in an emotional straightjacket.

Often we need help in recalling and applying the principles that can make a difference. In Chapter 2 we suggested you write down ideas you want to remember and carry them on a card for review. Why not do the same with these three steps? Add them to your list and keep looking at them until they are a part of you.

It's a good way to avoid life in an emotional straightjacket.

chapterFOUR

Worship and War at Church

In the past twenty years or so, an increasing number of pastors have been forced from their pulpits by the insidious manipulations and personal projections of troubled people. While the public usually expects the church to be peaceful, today it is often quite the opposite. Explosions can erupt out of nowhere, and members are swept away in the backwash of confusion and accusations. Often irate parishioners accuse pastors of some misbehavior, and before long the entire community is buzzing with hot gossip. On other occasions, churches split because a group of believers is angry over some direction the congregation is taking. Rather than finding a happy middle ground, a new church starts. The stories are endless. What in the world is going on?

The truth is, *difficult people go to church.*

Listening to sermons and reading the Bible creates the anticipation of a congregation populated by people who love God, each other, and strangers in need. The church should be a place of caring, attentive, forgiving people. We pray that those goals will prove to be universally true.

However, today's churches are filled with inquiring people seeking help and healing for their brokenness. They may stand at the altar and ask God's blessing as they commit themselves to new standards of behavior, but it may take a long time for many of these people to change. In the interim, they continue to bring their problems inside the church.

Collisions in the Congregation

Expect to find crazymakers in churches all over the world. Some aspects of church life seem to particularly draw them. In most churches, the people who pray the longest and sing the loudest also tend to be the most narcissistic. Most people naively think these attention-seekers are the most spiritual, but the opposite is usually true.

Janice was an unavoidably noticeable person in Rev. Frank Corbin's congregation. She was a difficult person with a problem of making statements that offended people. During a time of public prayer, Janice would often stand up and proclaim some admonition to the congregation that was supposedly a word from the Lord, and she often got herself and "the Lord" confused.

"If my people who are called by my name will listen to me," Janice would say aloud while everyone prayed, "I will come down from heaven, blessing them with an abundance that will overflow. Listen to my voice and you shall be blessed . . ." Unconsciously, she was thinking, *Listen to MY voice and all of you will see how "spiritual" I am.*

Those prayer messages came in the same forms, shapes, and sizes until the congregation could almost predict what they would hear. Occasionally a clash or misunderstanding followed with someone in the church over the issues in the prayers or something she said to someone. Janice appeared to want a special status in the congregation. Regardless of her spiritual pronouncements, Janice soon had a reputation for being a troublemaker.

"You know," Janice said forcefully during a Sunday school class, "I don't think our pastor knows what he's talking about on this idea of building a new fellowship hall. I believe we need a clear word from the Lord in order to go forward." (The "Lord," alias Janice.)

"Just a minute," another member replied with equal

strength. "Our pastor has been involved in this matter from the beginning and knows more about the issues than we do. The building is being built because some members of the congregation asked for it, and when the entire congregation was polled, they agreed that we needed more space."

Janice shrugged her shoulders. "I think he's trying to promote himself."

Boom! The battle was on and Janice had to back down. She had spoken insensitively again and gotten herself in trouble. Narcissists often "project" (like a slide projector) their own evil motives onto others. Matthew 7:3–5 addresses this common practice of seeing the "toothpick" in someone else's eye instead of the "log" in our own eye. This is projection, a common form of self-deceit. We *all* do it some. Narcissists just carry it to an extreme.

Difficult people often enjoy being in charge of the money and will seek positions on the Finance Committee where decisions are made about how to spend critical funds. If the church doesn't have a system of rotation where people only serve for a relatively short period of time, these individuals settle into power positions that can have a stranglehold on the life of the congregation. They feel they are doing God's work, but the rest of the church may feel they are bottlenecks!

The real issue? Crazymakers are at work.

Other Scenarios

Here's a typical clash of difficult people colliding in church. The conversation unfolded when Rev. Frank Corbin was leading a nominating committee meeting.

"Frank, I believe John Howell has been on the Finance Committee for five years and has worked with our church treasurer for some time," Mark Knapf said. "I feel he ought to be promoted to the Pastoral Relationship Committee that oversees the work of the clergy."

Frank bit his lip and hesitated. He knew John Howell had given considerable service to the church, but he had also seen Howell's encounters with other people. Pastor Corbin knew John Howell often dominated a meeting with pressure tactics. He feared Howell would create chaos if he began working with the church staff.

"I'd like to suggest that we promote him immediately," Knapf persisted.

"Thank you," Pastor Corbin said, "but I must confess that I have some reservations. I feel we should wait several months before we make any changes in the Pastoral Relationship Committee. Let's come back to this issue later."

"But," Knapf pushed, "I've already talked with John Howell about this very matter and heard him express a willingness to serve."

"I don't believe we should ever appoint a person who is jockeying for the position," Corbin retorted.

"Now, wait a minute, " Knapf protested. The discussion that followed quickly became heated.

The truth was Pastor Corbin had correctly identified John Howell as a difficult person with the ability to ruin a committee and damage the church. Howell's inflexibility was the problem. However, if you followed the conversation carefully, you probably noticed that the pastor also put himself in the controlling position to decide what would follow. While the pastor has biblical authority for leadership, the issue here was not theological, but physiological, pertaining to how the church, itself, operated as a whole.

Although it may not seem to be so, difficult people may also prove to be emotionally fragile as time goes by. At first, they tend to work their way up the chain of command in the congregation. They quickly read the structure for making decisions and can be quite adept at recognizing footholds on the way to the top. The problem is that about the time they reach a place of significant leadership, their fragility emerges. They may begin to complain, "The church doesn't meet my needs anymore." Often they will begin saying the pastor "isn't really preaching the Word like he once did." They develop an endless line of complaints. When the pastor is in need of their leadership, they announce "God has called me elsewhere" and out the door they go! God sure gets blamed innocently for a lot of narcissistic human decisions!

How crazy can it get? A church elder once believed he was so unique and spiritual that he should no longer work at his regular job. Quitting his position, the elder set out to raise enough support from naive church members so that he would be able to do the work of a full-time "prayer warrior" and pursue nothing but spiritual tasks. Eventually the man even ran for the governor of the state but failed miserably. Divorcing his wife, he left the church that had supported him to find people out there in the tall grass who were truly on his spiritual level. (He is still looking.)

Trouble in the Pulpit

A number of years ago, Robert Wise was the pastor of a church and thought the staff was totally happy with their positions and the way in which the program was unfolding. Little hints had been left here and there about aspects of issues that not everyone agreed with, but in private conversations each staff member assured him they weren't disturbed by any of these disagreements. Life seemed to be moving right down the track, as it should.

Out of nowhere, one of the members of the staff started exhibiting a defiant attitude and began acting in an obstinate manner to those who had authority over him. Again, Robert was assured the issue wasn't serious, and he went back to his personal ministry with confidence in the future of the church. The Christmas season came and a glorious service left everyone with tears in their eyes. Following the midnight service, the staff gathered in the sacristy and exchanged gifts. Robert and his wife left for their annual vacation over the holidays feeling positive about their friends on the staff.

When he returned ten days later, Robert went by the church to pick up his mail. While walking through the halls, he noticed office doors were open. Much to his shock, he discovered five of the staff members' offices were completely vacant. He looked through the totally empty rooms not quite able to determine where the furniture, the books, the pictures, the vestments, the mementos had gone! It took him several minutes to realize that these five offices had been totally cleaned out! *The staff was gone.*

When he opened the mail, Robert found a letter sent to the entire congregation from these five staff members, describing how they had been treated in a shabby, prejudiced, and harmful manner by the senior pastor (which was him). They were prepared to sue Robert and the church for the destructive treatment they had received at the hands of the tyrant who ran the place like a medieval dungeon. Robert stared at the letter as if it had come from another planet. He had no clue what was going on. Where in the world had this problem started?

Only weeks later after the smoke cleared did he get a straightforward picture of the fact that one of the staff had been spreading dissension for months. In fact, Robert found this person had a history of doing the same in other congregations. Staff members listened and grumbled among themselves without bringing these issues to the table. Even though they had all signed contracts calling for negotiation of disagreements, they walked out . . . because a crazymaker had whispered too many distracting words in their ears!

Sound familiar? Sure. Problems like this happen every day. While a congregation was worshiping, someone was preparing for war.

Eruptions often arise from the most unexpected sources. Pastors and their families can even be the origin of some of the problems. Frank Corbin is a good example of a difficult person called by God to do His work.

Way back in their college days, Alice Corbin had been drawn to Frank because of his devotion to the church. She soon discovered that he could get upset when things didn't work out the way he envisioned, but Alice believed time would rub off the rough edges.

During the years after seminary, Frank was employed as a member of a church staff. As an associate pastor, he was responsible for cultivating new members and working with the youth. Frank found the job exciting and fulfilling. His family seemed on its way to great things. A year later a child was born, and the Corbin household was a home of happiness and contentment. Unfortunately, there was more to the story.

Alice discovered that periodically Frank became irritated with what he considered a lack of efficiency at the church. Secretaries didn't perform with the skill he expected. When the pressure increased and the women proved to be slow and plodding, he became upset. Frank ended up barking at the secretaries and pushing them to work harder. Every couple of months Frank would become so angry that he would yell at the women.

Nancy, Frank's secretary, liked the Corbin family, but she had never worked for anyone who treated her with the seeming indifference she often received from Frank. Nancy started calling Alice and crying on her shoulder. Alice knew exactly what was troubling Nancy, since Alice had experienced Frank's anger and was aware of how unyielding he could be. One afternoon, Nancy called for help.

"He's done it again!" Nancy complained to Alice. "Frank just ripped me to shreds!"

Alice caught her breath and tried to reorder her thoughts. "I'm sorry to hear that happened," she said slowly. What could she say and still be loyal to her husband?

"Frank came into my office and was livid that I hadn't completed the typing for his Calling Committee meeting tonight. I told him the materials would be ready by five o'clock, but he wanted everything at that exact moment. I tried to explain, but he was relentless. The encounter was awful."

"I see. Did you have a legitimate reason for the problem?"

"Absolutely!" Nancy said. "The senior pastor asked me to finish typing a finance report, and I had to put his work first. That problem seemed to make Frank even angrier."

"And how did Frank's yelling make you feel, Nancy?"

Nancy thought for a moment. "Crazy," she said. "It made me feel like I was working in a loony bin."

Crazymakers and God

Could a pastor drive you over the edge? Sure. From the pulpit to the pew and back again, difficult people can be religious and attend church faithfully. Christian people have the same problems as everyone with psychological issues. In fact, difficult people may genuinely love God and still have a hard time relating to people. However, their attempts at spirituality don't earn them any exemptions for their insensitive behavior!

Near the beginning of the service in many churches, the congregation says a "Prayer of Confession." They admit out loud that they have not loved God and others as they should have. Most of us recognize that these public intercessions extend to frightening sins like fornication and stealing, but some of us don't feel these prayers are equally appropriate for being testy and overly critical. However, the truth is that our universal sinfulness means everyone has the capacity and tendency to be a difficult person. Certainly the prayer forces all of us to confess aloud so anyone listening can hear our repentance. Crazymakers should be in the pew on Sunday morning saying these prayers because they have business with God that needs to be straightened out.

Responding to Crazymakers

How should we react to these enigmas when we show up as peacemakers only to find war in the church?

First, expect problems and don't be shocked when they occur. The issues are normal, human, predictable, and manageable. Keep in your mind a realistic picture of how a church or any other social institution functions in a world where difficult people abound.

Second, stay informed about the dynamics occurring in these confrontations. Pastors, lay leaders, and the people sitting in the pew need to develop sensitivities for how problems develop. Reading books like *Crazymakers* will help create insight into the problems.

Discussion groups can help bring a depth of understanding about what is occurring. Staff members may talk together either informally or in a structured group about the difficult people in the church. They can take a look at the history of their encounters with these people and compare notes on what to do when situations twist out of hand. They may discover what sets a person off or learn a new way to deal with what irritates an insensitive crazymaker. In addition, they often discover how to minister to crazymakers without getting hooked into their issues. Insight will lead to adjustments that can diminish the problems. The more we know, the better equipped we will be to face confrontations!

Third, everyone needs spiritual preparation, and the Scripture offers us important insight into what to expect. Reading the book of Proverbs imparts critical direction. Proverbs 9:7–8 says, "He who corrects a scoffer gets shame for himself, and he who rebukes a wicked man only harms himself. Do not correct a scoffer, lest he hate you."

Proverbs suggests that we should avoid head-on collisions when possible because difficult persons tend to be even more hardheaded than we are! Our task is to find a way to come alongside these people with as gentle a word as possible. Often encouragement will accomplish more than confrontations.

Alice finally decided she had to confront Frank about the anger problem in the church office because it was both hurting the secretary and starting to affect Frank's reputation. He had to control his anger if he was going to have an effective ministry.

One evening when Frank was in a positive mood, Alice said, "I need to talk with you about a problem at the church. I need your counsel and advice."

"Sure," Frank said. "How can I help?"

"The issue has to do with a person who gets so angry that he attacks his secretary. Unfortunately, the word is starting to spread about his uncontrollable temper."

Frank blinked several times and took a deep breath. "You wouldn't be talking about me, would you?"

"Does it sound like you?" Alice asked.

For several moments Frank didn't say anything. His eyes moved back and forth as if he were taking a quick account of what he had just heard. "Yes," he finally said.

"You do get angry sometimes and say harsh things?"

"You know I do," Frank answered. "I wish I didn't, but at times matters get out of hand."

"I understand," Alice said, "and I'm not condemning you. I need your help to correct an important problem."

The stage was set for a solution. Alice had confronted Frank's problem in an oblique manner that didn't push him into a head-on collision. Frank knew Alice was right, and he was willing to examine the situation.

After thirty minutes of talking, Alice asked Frank to decide *how he would change* the environment at the church. He resolved to apologize to Nancy and to develop a new approach to the issues that upset him. He would pray and go for a walk around the block before talking to anyone about his irritations.

Fourth, we also need a different strategy when the difficult persons cannot be moved so easily. Jesus gave his followers an important and intelligent approach to such confrontations. In Matthew 18:15–17, He suggested we take two or three witnesses with us when confronting error. These witnesses provide a safe environment for discussing painful problems. Moreover, they also provide an accurate description of what was said; it is hard to spread false rumors when several people witnessed a discussion.

Directions for Difficult Days

No business, club, or institution can avoid difficult people. The church is the best place in the world to learn how to deal with these folks. Anticipate that you'll have to pay careful attention to your own responses. Here are a few final facts to remember.

FACTS TO REMEMBER

1. While churches are places of love and worship, don't minimize the confrontations when they occur. It's important to identify the difficult people when they surface.

2. Crazymakers can change, but they may have to be confronted. In order to maintain an atmosphere of peace and tranquillity for yourself and others, it may be your turn to wave the flag that stops their train.

3. Remember who is your source for the strength and tenacity needed to deal with difficult people. God is the foundation of our capacities. Let Him help you find strength for the hard times.

Don't forget—difficult days can turn into delightful times!

chapterFIVE

Employer or Egomaniac?

Allan Cole always came on strong when you first met him. He had a million one-liners and was constantly spinning jokes. When you walked away from talking with Allan, a single thought rumbled around in the back of your mind. *You know*, you would say to yourself, *Allan could really become my best friend! He feels like the sort of person I'd love to have in my life.*

Allan had the same effect when he showed up for a job. Because he was well educated, Allan always was a good candidate for getting hired in a managerial position. The employment personnel inevitably liked him, but not as much as his staff who thought he'd meet their highest expectations of a thoughtful boss. After a couple of months the scenery changed because Allan was a crazymaker.

Usually two to three weeks went by, and then people started noticing that Allan was actually argumentative. He particularly seemed to take issue when people expressed opinions contrary to his own. After a few discussions, Allan's conversational pattern was obvious. He appeared to listen, but he wasn't actually hearing what other people were saying. Instead Allan was waiting for an opportunity to attack, and once the exchange began, he wouldn't back down. The bottom line was *always* that Allan couldn't be wrong.

By the end of the first month, the staff began to get the picture. Employees either buckled under, or they were on their way out the door. No one could have any question about who was in charge of the office. All the trains ran through Allan's office or they got derailed!

Allan functioned as if employees had nothing else to do but keep him happy. Allan didn't allow any excuses. The work would get done or else! He dangled being fired over their heads as if the possibility were an invisible guillotine with the release cord tied to his desk.

No matter how much time employees had previously spent on the job, Allan's only concern was what they were doing *at the exact minute* he stood in front of their desks. One fire burned in his belly: The company would be number one or he would find new employees. Needless to say, excellent employees started looking elsewhere for a new job.

Allan was a crazymaker who lacked empathy for others.

Who Clogged the Mail Slot?

Trouble at the office spells tension in every other area of our world! No one likes to face the struggle that follows at home, with the kids, the friends, and everyone else in sight. We want to keep the letters coming and going without a clash occurring at the mailbox.

Most employees work because they need the income. Consequently, people don't quit unless the pain has become significant. In addition, when we end up in a collision with the boss, we usually don't get a letter of recommendation to help us get the next position. In other words, no one wants to go out the back door because the person in the front office doesn't like him or her.

But what do you do to endure the emotional abuse from an overbearing ogre? Unfortunately, too many supervisors use techniques that force workers to tiptoe over a bed of hot coals every day of the week. Sooner or later these strugglers must find a way out of the fire. What can they do?

Let's go back and take a second look at friendly old Allan Cole. What made him such a contradictory person, with smiles one day and frowns the next?

The Cole family would not have been a particularly inviting home for any of us to grow up in. Highly formal, Allan's father, Tom, directed family life like he was orchestrating a concert in Vienna where every member of the symphony was completely under his baton. He didn't allow for individual interpretation, but expected his view of the musical score to be followed with precision. Allan's mother, Harriet, knuckled under like the obedient first-chair violinist. She didn't want to get whacked on the head with the conductor's baton, so she did as she was told. However, Harriet periodically reached her limits and rebelled. Then the music abruptly changed to argumentative explosions! Allan wanted to hide from his father and his parents' verbal clashes.

From Harriet and Tom, the son learned how to smile ingratiatingly. Grinning certainly proved more effective than scowling. He developed a growing awareness that it was better to appear pleasing at the outset and worry about making his points later in the game. Both his smile and his delayed attack tactic were developed from adjusting to his father's stringent demands.

Because he never gained any sense of his true capacities, Allan kept a simmering fear of his inabilities cooking on the back burner. At any moment, his father could reach over and smash him. Consequently, Allan feared other people might always trump his cards, even if he played aces. Allan lacked any sense of the size of his own strength.

The bottom line? Allan had a control problem, just as all other crazymakers. Allan didn't have a sense of how badly he afflicted others with his heavy-handedness, because he didn't feel their pain. His ultimate concern was making sure he could keep his hands on the controls.

When Self-Esteem and Empathy Go Down the Drain

Another way to describe Allan's problem would be to say that he lacked self-confidence. He came on so strong because he couldn't envision any other way of conveying his feelings, except pushing people against the wall and shouting. Often the more inferior people feel unconsciously, the more superior they act consciously.

When people have not received the normal love and care they need as children, a vacuum is formed in their emotions. Often, it is like a void in their souls. They don't have a clear idea of how other people hurt, worry, cry, struggle, and anguish over the most common situations. A loss of this empathy results in a diminished ability to care for other people.

One of the modern villains of the screen is Hannibal Lector, the psychopathic psychiatrist. In *Silence of the Lambs* we meet this frightening criminal who appeared to be normal and at times sensitive. He was an epicurean and a gourmet cook. With a genius mind, Lector remembered and recognized amazing facts about people. The problem was he wanted to kill and eat them.

Hannibal Lector felt nothing but his own needs, drives, desires, and peculiar ambitions. The psychiatrist loved no one and totally lacked empathy. And that's why *the villain is so terribly frightening to us.*

Of course, a difficult person is light years away from a crazy Hannibal Lector, but the basic problem is the same. In one of his most frightful moods, Allan Cole could seem a monster to the people he was hurting. When you're on the receiving end, cold people can freeze you out.

Trying to Fix the Brokenness

If we are going to help difficult people, we need to get in touch with our own lack of self-confidence. Even the most robust of us have times when we feel deeply inadequate; great athletes confess their many times of weakness, as do successful politicians.

Think about it for a moment. Can you remember a period in your life when you felt defeated? Go back to those feelings of emptiness and remember how hollow they were.

For example, many years ago, Robert Wise went through a disastrous church experience while serving as a pastor. While he hadn't done anything wrong, he was caught up in a bewildering set of circumstances that caused him to keep his mouth shut until he sank in the whirlpool of despair, dragging everyone else to the bottom. Today, when he wants to get in touch with feelings of helplessness and hopelessness, Robert goes back to those days and the months that followed.

Within a matter of seconds, Robert can remember wanting to hide; he can feel the depression that nagged at him. He once again knows the pain of not being sure what to do and not being understood by people who at one time had been his friends. The despair again fills his mind.

While we may want to kill people like Allan Cole when they are chewing on us, we need to get in touch with *what they are feeling.* Fear is behind their anger. Rather than hitting them in the mouth, we need to reassure them. Consider this surprising conversation in Allan Cole's office.

"I've told you a thousand times," Allan bore down on the woman sitting in front of him, "don't let this work pile up on you! You won't be able to get it done by five o'clock."

"I understand, Mr. Cole." His assistant kept smiling. "You look tired and under a considerable amount of strain."

"What?" Cole frowned.

"You seem worn. Is everything all right?"

"Certainly," Allan barked. "I don't look that bad!" he snapped.

"No." The assistant didn't stop smiling. "But you sound like someone has been on your case and you are irritated with the whole world."

Allan stepped back. "I . . . I . . . don't understand."

She looked at Allan sympathetically. "It's okay. We all have tough days. Don't worry. I'll get this work done for you." She turned back to the computer and started typing again.

For a moment Allan Cole stood in front of her desk staring; then he walked off with a strange look creeping across his face. The bomb had been defused because the assistant had carefully avoided the crunch Allan was trying to put on her. Let's analyze what occurred.

Duck, Bob, and Weave

Amateur boxers have developed a style that has proven successful in the ring. Rather than attack, they attempt to be defensive and counterpunch. In a similar way, we need to learn how to avoid emotionally frigid people like Allan Cole when they come flying across the canvas at us. We might call this approach a "side-step alternative." Here's what you need to remember:

1. Duck. Don't let difficult people hit you with their cold insensitivity. Remind yourself *they have a problem*. While there may be an issue between the two of you, the impact you feel when they come crashing toward you began in their own high-strung orientation.

Look a difficult person in the eye, and say to yourself, *This person's hurt is coming out as anger*. Remind yourself to take a sidestep approach to the attack. Your silent inner conversation will help you avoid getting disoriented by what the person says. The process builds a fence around you.

The trick is not to take their actions personally. You must condition yourself to instantly recognize it is "their" problem. Often Paul Meier will imagine himself to be a third person, standing beside himself and the crazymaker, analyzing the situation. When he was five years old, a bully pushed Paul into the snow and ran off. Paul got up and walked over to his mother. Brushing himself off, he said, "I wonder why the boy did that to me?"

Paul instinctively knew the only answer was the other boy's aggressive behavior, which was prompted by something in this child's personality.

Get the idea? That's the approach we want you to learn to take.

2. *Bob.* "Bobbing" is a technique of moving up and down in short quick motions so you are not an easy target. You do this emotionally by offering alternatives as the assistant did with Allan. She suggested that he looked tired and seemed to be worn out. Rather than take the defensive, she offered sympathetic understanding. It's rather hard to hit such a moving target!

She could also have said, "Allan, you know that I always get my work done on time. Something else must be bothering you. Are you upset with some other problem in the office?"

You may think that talking to a superior in this manner sounds arrogant, but when the question is asked with genuine caring, it isn't. An honest question, centered on the other person's well-being, is another example of bobbing.

3. *Weave.* The assistant might have said, "Allan, I only have eight hours in the day, and I can't do all of this work. Would you like to choose what I should do for the rest of the day?" This would have forced Allan to create a plan, weaving the assistant away from his offensive. When you offer the attacker an option and *make this person decide* what to do, that's a weave. You want to give the crazymaker an alternative.

But be ready with a backup alternative, based on the amount of time you have to work, just in case your own crazymaker insists on a plan you cannot fulfill.

In these alternatives it is also important to confront the supervisor until he or she has made a choice. At some point you may need to say, "I'm sorry. I can't do what you are asking. Maybe we need to call in a negotiator and see what he would say."

The point? You're trying to avoid getting hit! Of course, this approach takes practice. Boxers certainly get knocked down as they learn how to duck, bob, and weave. Don't be afraid of making a mistake. Instead, jump in and discover how to be more skillful.

The Bottom Line

When you are dealing with people who have limited emotional capacity to feel what is happening inside others, you cannot expect to appeal to their sense of caring. You must find some other way to get around them, like the sidestep alternatives discussed in the previous section.

But what happens when the employer is truly a full-blown narcissist and won't respond to kindness or options? Then it's time to make a decision. You must ask yourself how badly you need this particular job. There are employers out there who aren't worth the wear and tear they put on their employees. When you hit one of those types, it is time to hang up your spurs and go on down the road to the next corral. It isn't the only job in town. (We would suggest you find another job before you quit, since most of us need the income and other companies like to hire *working* people, not unemployed people.)

One of Jesus' teachings is that in following Him, you are to count the cost. Your place of work ought also to be a place of serving God. When you can't serve your Lord effectively, the cost has become too great. You need to find another job, but before you do . . . see if you can defrost the boss.

chapterSIX

When the Puppy Turns into a Bear

Crazymakers have a unique way of spreading confusion. Because they blindside us, their initial assault comes as a surprise. Reeling from the attack, we find ourselves struggling to understand what we've done wrong. In that interim of reflection, the confrontation escalates and nothing makes sense. When the attack comes from a highly narcissistic person, it is even more confusing. Where do we turn?

We need to learn how to identify the *real problem* going on behind the flying words and threatening fists. They aren't going to tell us what's in the back of their minds, so we must learn how to read between the lines, hear the unspoken words, and recognize the unseen dimensions of their behavior. Identifying their problem is crucial to making progress. Don't spiritualize the problem. Consider how this difficulty tripped up Sally Harris.

For the past decade Sally Brown Harris has been an elementary schoolteacher, working with fourth-grade children. problems she had in the classroom with difficult kids were nothing compared to what Sally battled at home. Her husband George's completely unpredictable behavior often produced angry eruptions when Sally least expected it. Most of the time, the Harris children lived in terror of what might occur when the whole clan gathered around the evening supper table. One summer evening this typical conversation occurred.

"Would you please pass the bread?" ten-year-old Joan asked her brother, Andrew.

"Sure." Andrew picked up the plate and handed it to his sister.

"Did you remember to buy new tires for the car yesterday?" Sally asked George.

George froze in place. "What tires?" He sounded slightly ruffled.

"You know." Sally smiled. "Several days ago we talked about how thin the treads were on our tires and you promised to have new ones put on. Those old tires were really a safety problem."

"I don't know what you're talking about," George growled.

"Come on, honey," Sally answered. "You promised that you would . . ."

"And now you're trying to make me look like a fool," George cut her off. "Don't put your nonsense on me, Sally. This is only another example of your forgetting to do something." His voice became louder.

The children stared into their dinner plates, and Sally looked shocked.

"Now, wait a minute," Sally said. "I was only trying to find out if . . ."

"If you could run our lives by remote control," George snapped. "Always nagging, aren't you? Keep this up and we'll have a real big-time war going right here at the supper table." George glared at Sally as if he were ready to climb across the table and assault her with his fork.

Sally's mouth dropped. In a few words she and her husband had gone from a simple question to a major assault. Tears welled up in her eyes.

What in the world was going on? At the least, Sally failed to identify the fundamental problem operating in her husband's mind. Her simple question made George feel inadequate because it revealed that he had missed doing something he had agreed to do. He wasn't talking about tires, but his own sense of importance and capacity. George had mentally shifted gears and was on to a new fight. Rewriting history!

George Harris was attempting to restructure a previous

conversation by denying that it ever happened. Once he rewrote how the lines should read, Sally was supposed to say in effect, "Oh, now I understand. Let me start again."

George wanted her to ignore reality and buy in to his view of events, which would change the whole scenario. He didn't *really forget* to buy the tires. Sally should agree the conversation didn't happen and then life could be happy again. Sounds normal enough . . . if you're driving on the crazy side of the street.

No. If Sally was going to stay in touch with reality, she must not let George change the past. She had to identify why she was unable to do so.

The Root of Sally's Problem

Sally's problems actually started decades ago in her hometown of Billings, Montana. The peaceful setting of the neighborhood always tilted on a fine line because Sally's father had a habit of coming home drunk. Even though Bill Brown wasn't a bad man when sober and often helped people in the neighborhood, he simply couldn't stay away from the liquor store. When he was drunk, Bill Brown could be extremely difficult and he had a habit of picking fights. He wasn't above slapping Sally's mother. On more than one occasion, Bill had gone after Sally. She had grown up in a home where fights, altercations, and unpredictable behavior were expected.

When Sally Brown met teetotaling George Harris, she didn't realize that he was actually a great deal like Bill Brown. Although he always stayed sober, George's temperament was much like a "dry" drunk. By the midpoint in her marriage, she had come to expect chaos and confusion, which were very similar to what her father had created.

When she was a small child, Sally had unconsciously concluded that the insatiable explosions in her home simply had to be *her fault*. That singular conclusion continued on into the future, and when she became Mrs. George Harris, the same idea persisted. What was wrong in the Harris household? Her conclusion was clear: *it was Sally Brown Harris*.

Sally's unexamined conclusion put her in an impossible position. She turned the anger that erupted from the fights with George in upon herself, and she ended up becoming deeply depressed. Eventually Sally reached the point where she would often not buckle up her car's seat belt because Sally honestly felt she would be better off dead. Maybe a car wreck would bring the whole mess of black emotions to a quick finish!

Why Marry George?

Sally Brown's first interest in George began in college. Back in those Ivy League days, George was a handsome guy and a popular campus figure. People enjoyed his friendly nature, like a warm and playful puppy. As Sally observed him, George was obviously quite capable and a good student leader. She was particularly attracted to him because of his interest in a Christian vocation. They eventually began attending a Bible study on campus, and a romantic relationship developed.

Having grown up around the church, Sally had some knowledge of the Bible, but her insight was limited. The college Bible studies helped add some important components. However, she never really developed a well-informed faith. From this meager background, Sally Brown formed what would prove to be a significant idea for the future. Somewhere along the way, she decided that it was the wife's responsibility to be *completely obedient to her husband* (which is not a biblical perspective). That decision, coupled with the struggles in her childhood home, pushed Sally Brown into the desire of becoming a completely compliant wife married to a totally dominating husband.

During their wedding, Sally asked the minister to make one change in the service. Before God, she wanted to pledge complete obedience. George Harris beamed. His dreams were coming true, but at a price Sally wouldn't have thought possible. The cute little puppy named George was going to grow up and become a real bear with claws!

Sally's conscious mind had "fallen in love" with George because she thought he was a cute little puppy. But her co-dependent, unconscious mind sensed that he was truly a hostile, controlling bear who was just like the father she always felt responsible to fix. As Tina Turner's famous old song says, "what's love, but a second-hand emotion!"

When the Fangs Start to Grow

Disagreements are inevitable in any marriage, Sally realized. At first, she bowed to George's pressure and gave in. After several years, disagreements developed that weren't so easily solved, and when the children started arriving, the tensions escalated.

Sally discovered that when she firmly opposed George, his nostrils flared and his eyes hardened. If she continued to push back, George only became more obstinate. He expected to be the steamroller over a wife who was the asphalt pavement! Even though she tried to avoid arguments, Sally found that she couldn't be nearly as passive as she had hoped. George Harris wasn't interested in being right as much as he was determined to stay in a position of control. The stage was set for painful battles! He even tried to control her mannerisms and her personal interests as he controlled the thermostats in the house.

Self-absorbed, narcissistic people need to stay in the driver's seat, buy the gasoline, keep the credit cards, hold on to the receipts, manage the pocketbook, validate expenditures, have all the trains run through their offices, check the luggage, approve the tickets, fly the airplane, and keep the radio on their favorite station. They are "in-charge-Marge" women and "hold-the-reins-Randy" men.

They will dominate!

While Sally believed she only had a different opinion from her husband, George saw their disagreements as acts of rebellion. Once agitated, he lowered his fangs. At that point, their disagreements started moving toward disasters.

Identifying the Problem

Once their quarrels became head-on collisions, Sally knew she needed help. Because her background had programmed her to assume she was the source of the entire problem, Sally went alone to a counselor to seek insight on what she was doing wrong. A professional might help her clarify why the man she deeply loved could elicit such throbbing pain.

During the first sessions, Sally agonized over why the smallest issues created angry confrontations. The counselor kept probing the nature of the Harris's conflicts. It wasn't until the third session that he hit pay dirt.

"Do you feel that there is any one area in which George's demands are unrealistic?" the counselor asked.

Sally looked down at the floor and appeared embarrassed. "I . . . I . . . really hate to say," she said slowly.

"However, we seem to have one constant argument . . . that I feel is really a sign of George's being unfair."

The counselor smiled. "Don't be afraid to be forthright. We're here to sort the problem out."

Sally took a deep breath. "George constantly gripes that our sex life isn't adequate. The truth is that George presents this area of our marriage in a totally unrealistic light. I can tell you that he is simply flat wrong when he complains about a 'limited' sexual life. We are already far beyond what is considered normal in most marriages."

"Hmm," the counselor thoughtfully drummed on the desk with the tips of his fingers. "Are there any other areas in which George complains about limits?"

Sally thought for a moment. "Well . . . I hadn't thought of it . . . in quite this light . . . but George isn't happy about how money is spent. He constantly complains that I spend too much when the truth is that I never go beyond our budget, but he spends large amounts on boats and other things without even asking for my opinion. He thinks that since he earns most of the money, he should spend it however he wants. He's like a broken record on that subject."

For a few moments the counselor quietly reflected on what he had been hearing. Finally he asked, "Do you see any relationship between his complaints about your spending too much money and what he calls his 'limited' sex life?"

Sally frowned. "I don't think so. Money and sex are a long way apart."

"Yes," the counselor said thoughtfully, "but what issue is George actually complaining about? What's hiding behind the curtains?"

Sally kept frowning and looked perplexed. "I can't see where you are going with this. There's really no relationship that . . ." Sally stopped abruptly. "Oh, yes! The issue that's at the heart of the matter is George's desire to dominate all the decisions. He's the one who wants to be in charge of everything that happens. *George wants to be in control!*"

The Heart of the Matter

When we confront argumentative, self-absorbed narcissists, we must be ready for them to move their big guns into action because they will attempt to take control of the battlefield. Even though they may come up with good data during the disagreement, their opposition is only a symptom of their real concern. The bottom line is *controlling the discussion.*

Crazymakers are attempting to *manipulate the past* when they rewrite history. They have an unexamined idea of their own omnipotence, causing them to believe they can reach inside previous events and turn them around, like a potter working with a piece of clay until it takes the shape he wishes. These men and women have no sense of how bizarre their actions are. Without reflecting on what they are doing, these people change the facts around as a playwright does in rewriting a script. Of course, the rest of us stand there with our heads spinning, feeling as though we've been dropped in an insane asylum.

Sally began to notice that George had a strange, un-expected trait. When they came to the end of an argument, he would insist on having the last word even if the actual comment was trivial or meaningless.

After thirty minutes of heated exchange, Sally said angrily, "Look George, let's drop the matter. We aren't get-ting anywhere arguing about this subject."

"I'll accept that response as your admitting you are wrong."

"I didn't make any such admission. I said let's quit."

"Okay. I win," George insisted.

"If you say so, George. Let's drop it."

"I win," George insisted.

"I'm not talking about anyone prevailing."

"I accept your apology," George pushed.

"Please!" Sally pleaded.

"Please? Did I just hear an acceptance?"

Endless comments would go on and on until Sally stopped answering or left the room. After counseling, Sally began to see what was happening. The insistence on the last word was George's way of *staying in control to the bitter end . . .* no matter what the cost.

With time Sally Harris learned that she had to climb a series of steps if she was to find her way out of these battles with her husband. You might find these same rungs to be of importance in your struggles.

Step 1: What is the real issue? Sally discovered that the first step in coming to grips with the conflicts at home was to recognize that control was almost always the major issue hiding in the shadows. Even though the contents of the argument might be important, she had to recognize that George intended to be the master of the confrontation. Sally had to remember to stay focused on George's basic problem, regardless of what they were arguing about. George's fundamental personal issue was his need to be in control of the situation.

After you have been through one of these free-for-alls with a crazymaker, go back and attempt to write out the conversation exactly as it occurred. Do your best to get the flow of the argument down as it happened. Take the transcript and start reading it out loud. Read it over and over until you have a firm sense of the flow and dynamic of how the confrontation unfolded. Eventually, you will begin to develop your own sense of the inner issues operating behind the words. The undercurrents of the crazymaker's behavior will become clearer. These are the issues you want to identify. The better you can understand the difficult person's inner agenda, the more able you will be to respond without stepping into his or her minefield.

Step 2: Do you feel inadequate? When a difficult person is bearing down on you, you may intuitively feel he or she has gained the edge and stripped away your ability to be forceful. The next step is to recover your own sense of worthiness. Even though the other person's voice may be loud and forceful, you are not necessarily relegated to the backseat in the argument. The issue of using volume to dominate was a problem in the Harris family.

When George bore down on her, Sally always began to feel inadequate. Her lost sense of capability made it even more difficult for her to hold her ground. She had to remind herself that she hadn't necessarily lost the upper hand. In the midst of conflict, Sally needed to emotionally take a step backwards and get a deep breath. Unwinding from the immediate screaming and hollering always helped her gain an inner sense of stability. Once her equilibrium was restored, she gained the balance necessary to remain focused.

Take a calm look at yourself. Reread your transcript and notice points in your explosive conversations where you felt inadequate. This allows you to identify what buttons the crazymaker punches with you. Once you know what causes you to retreat, you will be able to find different ground to stand on.

No matter what you feel your inadequacies are, try not to feel defensive. All of us have developed areas in our lives where we are sensitive. Our pasts have pitfalls that affect us. Everyone has been there and gotten a T-shirt to prove it. That's normal, natural, and unavoidable.

Step 3: What lit the fuse? Usually we have no sense of the dynamic that set off a self-absorbed person, but there are definitely "buttons" that we pushed to send off the rockets. We must learn to identify what crosses the line with this type of person.

Sally learned that George didn't like to be caught off guard. The "new-tires-war" started because Sally identified a responsibility in which he had come up short, and she caught him on the blind side. For many narcissistic people, being wrong feels like being inadequate, and they start to defend themselves from an attack that doesn't actually exist!

Consider the narcissists' needs. What areas of sensitivity start his or her pursuit of power and control? Does he fret over whether all the doors are locked because he worries about keeping your home under control? Is he always watching how you dress to make sure you don't offend anyone out there on the street? Or periodically does she correct your speech because she is worried that you may not come across as intelligent?

Many times the issues narcissists worry about are small, but the pressure can mount and an insignificant problem may feel like a boulder dropped on your front porch. Often they are attempting to protect weakness that they may camouflage quite well. Nevertheless, if you start listening for what's lurking behind the scenes, you can start to recognize the triggers that spell danger.

Writing down old arguments can help you crawl inside the mind of a crazymaker. The transcript gives you a form you can reread and study for clues. Often we must review these collision issues if we are to get some sense of what is truly going on in the confrontations. People must spend some time with what they have written in note form before the problem fully crystallizes for them. Don't be discouraged if it takes time to make a breakthrough into insight. The important thing is coming to a full knowledge of the truth.

A Helpful Conclusion

Sally's struggles have given us three important questions we can learn to ask ourselves when we confront difficult people.

1. What is the real issue?

2. Do I feel inadequate?

3. What lit the fuse?

These queries will help you sort out substance from flash and fury. At the outset, remember not to take these issues lightly. They are important. When puppies grow up and turn out to be bears, you must not minimize the issues. Bears bite much harder than puppies!

One issue must be kept clearly in mind. Bears are concerned with *power and control*. They won't give up easily on those two areas and may be willing to die rather than give in! *You must learn* to sidestep the two minefields when struggling with the self-absorbed.

chapterSEVEN

Bedlam in the Backyard

During Sally Harris's visits with her counselor, she was challenged to consider what was the most important element in her marriage to George. One of the areas she identified was a high commitment to achieving a meaningful family life for her entire family. Her children Kim, Joan, and Andrew were the delights of her life, and Sally didn't want to do anything that might block the kids' development. In fact, she was willing to bend over backwards to create the most positive family life possible. But it was not easy.

During her many confrontations with George, Sally recognized the depth and ferocity of her husband's anger. Sally wasn't sure what the issues were, but she knew the problem was serious. While Sally didn't intend to turn into a mouse, scurrying around the house doing only what "the boss" ordered, she also didn't want to be the source of his temper explosions. Remembering the times when her father had physically abused her, Sally certainly didn't want to push George into a physical confrontation.

After several counseling sessions, Sally began reading both Christian and secular books that helped shed light on the family problems. Several weeks of talking and reading led Sally to an important conclusion. Regardless of what George did, she was going to become an emotionally healthy person.

Getting Stronger!

Sally's counselor was delighted with the decision. Facing the old issues from her past home life in Montana and confronting her emotional needs would help Sally walk on a better path. In addition, she would learn to think more creatively about the struggles that periodically erupted in the Harris household.

Sally began to discover the importance of self-discipline. As the truth about her own emotional makeup emerged, Sally had to make difficult changes. Consistent attention to her nervous and compliant reactions in an argument began to change her responses. However, these adjustments did not produce overnight miracles. Her struggles with George continued to be a persistent problem. Sally's recovered competence did not mean that her bear would turn back into a puppy!

One of Sally's most important discoveries was her realization that it was acceptable to become angry. Her father, Bill Brown, had always overreacted to any show of emotion on her part when she was a child; therefore Sally Brown grew up being afraid of her own feelings. When she became Sally Harris, the reservations came with her.

The counselor helped Sally recognize that much of her depression came from unexpressed anger, which she feared releasing. Anger, he said, is a normal reaction to conditions that violate us. When Sally repressed her feelings, the hostility only disguised itself as self-abasement. Sally discovered the need to allow herself to experience the full range of whatever she felt. This recognition prepared Sally to face a turning point in her relationship with George.

During Saturday lunch, George announced to the family that he was expecting six people over for supper *that evening*. It was important to make a good impression on these people, he said, so he wanted the family to put their best foot forward. He expected the children to be well-dressed, and Sally's supper should be considerably above average.

Looking straight into Sally's eyes, George said, "I don't want any runaway emotionalism. Understood?"

Sally blinked several times. "Of course," she answered. "That's not my style."

George snorted. "You kids need to make me look good. Everyone got it?"

Joan nodded her head. "Yes, sir."

"Good!" George put his napkin on the table. "Andrew, let's go outside and throw the football around. We need to get out of your mother's way."

"It would have been nice to have known about this dinner a week ago," Sally said.

George made no response and walked out.

Sally looked at Joan, and they exchanged a knowing look. Obviously, she would be preparing the meal by herself. Sally pushed back from the table and went into the kitchen. She made herself note that her husband's personal comments were unfair, as well as his giving her a last-minute command to not only feed but also impress a group of people. It made her angry. Sally let herself feel the hostility.

George's surprise supper announcement had caught Sally completely off guard, and she wasn't sure what to fix. She picked up a cookbook and started thumbing through the pages. Thirty minutes later she had an idea of what she would throw together. At that moment Sally heard a noise out on the back porch and leaned over to look out the kitchen window.

Apparently Andrew had missed the football, and it bounced against the house. She watched George charge his son, bouncing him off the porch wall. Andrew reached up and flipped his father on the ear to push him back. Sally instantly saw the look on George's face. Andrew had violated his father's space, and it hadn't set well. Just as she feared, George abruptly pushed his son backwards with a hard shove.

Andrew turned sideways, letting the force of the shove slide away. In an instant reaction, he whirled back around and gave his father a hard push. George bounced backward and tripped over a short planter filled with geraniums. He went sprawling backwards on the grass.

Sally caught her breath. She realized the fall meant George wasn't in control of the situation. He would come up like a wounded bull! To her horror, Sally watched George leap up, ready to land a knockout punch. She ran for the back door.

By the time Sally got outside, George had his son up against the house, and a full-blown fight had exploded. She rushed to get between the two, but Andrew was now as angry as his father. He made one wild swing that missed George, but the father landed a hard punch in the center of Andrew's chest, knocking the wind out of him.

"Stop it!" Sally screamed. "Don't hit each other!"

George jabbed her with the edge of his palm, sending Sally back into the porch wall. At the same moment, Andrew picked up a baseball bat. George grabbed the bat and slung his son backwards on the lawn. With a mighty heave, George lifted the bat over his head like an ax.

Sally screamed at the top of her voice and George stopped. He turned his head and looked at her, almost as if he might hit Sally with the baseball bat.

"Don't!" Sally yelled. "Don't hit anybody!"

George froze in place for a moment and then slowly lowered the bat. Andrew kept holding the side of his arm up over his face to protect his head. George looked back at his son as if he were still considering busting him. Finally George straightened up and lowered the bat to his side. Sally hadn't moved and kept watching him with fear in her eyes.

George started walking away. He took ten steps and then suddenly hurled the bat into the side of the garage door with a terrible crunch, leaving the bat stuck in the door. Then he disappeared around the side of the house.

Sally slowly walked away from the wall. By this time Andrew was standing, but his hands were shaking. Sally hugged him.

"I'm sorry," she said. "I'm so terribly sorry this happened."

Andrew didn't say anything. He silently went back into the house and shut the door behind him.

Sally plopped down into the canvas yard chair and started sobbing. This time George had gone way, way too far. She wasn't going to accept his outrageous behavior anymore. He was going to change or else. Her recovered emotional health had given Sally the strength to live beyond her fears!

What Went Wrong?

Let's shift our examination of roles for a moment and take a look at the problem from George Harris's side. Sally had been undergoing a number of personal changes that George couldn't understand. From his point of view, Sally was becoming increasingly difficult. He wasn't sure why, but she wasn't responding as he had always expected. It was difficult for him to keep the family on a basis that felt sound and stable, which made George feel anxious.

George had been raised in a family with high demands. His parents expected him to be in church every Sunday and made it clear they wouldn't tolerate any nonsense. They always pushed him to make good grades at school and wouldn't accept a poor performance. A negative behavior in public always resulted in a hard spanking at home. By the time he reached adulthood, George always felt that hidden inner push to perform at a higher level than he often felt capable of reaching. But he was good at a party. Always making quick, funny comments, George gave the appearance of a fun-loving extrovert. The truth was he actually felt uncertain and fearful that his world would spin out of control at any moment. Life was much harder for George than he let anyone know.

George's problem was *misplaced feelings*. He often didn't really know what he felt. The only clear fact was that succeeding was paramount. In the home he grew up in, George didn't see much love and compassion, but he did know how important accomplishment was. His father had impressed that on him.

One afternoon in childhood, young George was working in the back of his father's store in Salida, Kansas. A long, narrow hallway led from the alley to the back of the hardware store. He was sweeping the dirt and dust up off the cement when his father came back to check things out.

"You doing a good job?" Al asked the eight-year-old boy in a harsh voice.

Little George looked up. "Yes, sir."

Al Harris walked up and down the hall, staring at the corners and along the edges of the wall. "You're missing a lot," Al complained. "Why can't you do better?" He pointed to the wall. "You need to do this over again."

George bit his lip and nodded his head. "Yes, sir."

"I'm paying you to do a good job," Al said. "Don't want no halfway stuff back here."

"Yes, sir," George said and picked up the broom to start again.

Al started walking back to the front of the store but stopped before he got out of the hallway and came back. He reached over and put his hand on George's shoulder. "I'm not trying to be hard on you, son," he said with a hint of gentleness in his voice. "People expect good work. That's what will get you ahead in this world. Hard work is more important than anything else in life." Al slapped George on the back. "Remember that fact!" He walked out with a long, certain stride.

Little George didn't forget.

Years later in his own home, George couldn't understand why his family didn't seem to recognize how important it was to do things right. Half the time his daughter Joan acted like she was afraid of him, and periodically Andrew turned into a wildcat and fought with him. Of course, this behavior made George angry because all he was doing was what his father had done with him. He only wanted his children to know what counted. Probably his wife's blubbering pushed everything over the edge. He loved Sally, but she seemed to oppose him too often.

The problem? George's deepest feelings were entirely misplaced.

Because crazymakers have such strong power and control issues, they will stay in the driver's seat, regardless of what occurs. George saw his objective of creating a productive son and daughter as more important than how they felt about what he was doing to them.

Difficult people are committed to staying in the driver's seat at all cost. Consequently, crazymakers can be extremely disruptive and painful when they are sure their efforts are only the best for all concerned. When they crash into a tree, self-absorbed people simply get out and take a taxi to their next stop. They function almost as if they are programmed to drive straight ahead until their motor burns out.

But Sally had other ideas.

She had come to realize that the *regardless* in George's world had to be turned into *caring*. Sally believed that relationships were more important than accomplishments and that put her on a very different path. Her definition of her children's well-being was much broader than George's. After the Saturday afternoon battle between George and Andrew, Sally concluded that matters had to change. She was perfectly willing to let George drive the car, but she became determined her family would not suffer another crash at his hands.

Setting New Boundaries

With the help of what she had been reading and learning from the counselor, Sally concluded it was time to alter how they did business as a family. She had learned that boundaries were an extremely important part of showing and maintaining respect within the family circle. Lines of demarcation defined where aggressive behavior stopped. Boundaries place limits on what may be said or done in order to avoid harm. Sally set out to establish limits on what was permitted in the Harris family. She had taken a new and important step forward.

Crazymakers are hard to stop and usually their victims feel ill equipped to slow them down. Nevertheless, if peace is going to be restored, someone must enforce the rules. When spouses discover they are married to crazymakers, they must learn to use boundaries and enforce them. The problem is that the individuals under attack are reluctant to stand up to the adversary. They may feel weak and already browbeaten. Regardless of the negative emotion, here are some guidelines to help set up boundaries that can improve relationships.

1. *The boundary must be appropriate and realistic.* You cannot ask for a condition that places stringent demands on the other person that would not be held as acceptable by an objective source. For example, telling your spouse to mow the lawn more often or you will move to a motel won't work. Telling your mate to run the dishwasher once a day whether it is full or not would not be considered reasonable. Likewise, it would be unacceptable to tell a child to practice the piano every day or lose access to your computer forever. However, when you are confronted by violent or excessive confrontation, you have the right to refuse to be treated in a demeaning and harmful manner.

2. *The boundary and the alternative must be clearly stated.*

Think through *exactly* what behavior must stop, and state it in terms that the other person *completely* understands. Rather than being accusative or personal, your conditions should be declared in an objective form with the consequences defined *precisely*.

After the guests left on Saturday night, Sally confronted George. In as gracious a tone as she could muster, Sally firmly told him there would be no more physical exchanges. No matter how angry he became, she would not tolerate physical abuse in any form. If it happened again, she and the children would legally separate for as long as necessary, even indefinitely if needed.

George was shocked, but the firmness in Sally's voice communicated she meant business. The physical battles were over, and George would either conform to this boundary or he would no longer have a family. He started to get angry, but the intense stare in Sally's eyes told him this area was not even open for negotiation. Sally Harris had planted a "stop sign" in front of George's face.

The conditions and results were obvious.

3. You must resolutely be prepared to stand behind the stated conditions. A boundary is meaningless if there's no fence! You've got to be the hedgerow if crazymaking behavior is going to change. Before you state a boundary, you must know you will uphold your conditions, regardless of the backlash.

Sally reached the end of her tolerance when George physically attacked their son and then pushed her backward. A week later, George brought up the incident in the backyard for the first time. Looking defiant, he said to Sally, "I don't know what was so bad about that little skirmish last Saturday afternoon." Sally leaned forward, looked him squarely in the eye, and replied, "If it ever happens again, you won't have a family." George got the point for sure! You've got to stand on the same firm ground.

Facing the Impossible Issues

Drs. Meier and Wise believe in the sanctity of marriage. They will do everything possible to help prevent divorce in troubled marriages. However, they also recognize that when a person's physical or emotional well-being is threatened, strong action must be taken. If boundaries are put in place, and the spouse doesn't respect them, then separation and self-protection make sense.

Sound strong? It is! But strong medicine is the only variety that will cure the narcissistic crazymakers in your world. Here are some more additions for those cards you are carrying around with you. Keep these rules in mind because they are important for your well-being.

FACTS TO REMEMBER

1. Difficult people tend to be oblivious to your feelings. Expect them to be more concerned with themselves.

2. You must set the boundaries and enforce them if you want genuine change.

3. Even though the crazymaker is your spouse, don't anticipate that he or she will change overnight. You've got to maintain the boundaries necessary for your best interest.

Do these boundaries work? They worked for Sally Brown Harris. George got the message and the physical attacks ended.

chapter EIGHT

And What About the Kids?

Let's take a look at the Littleton family. These crazymakers have a twenty-one-year-old daughter, Amy, who is off at college, and a son, Jeff, who still lives at home. Amy and Jeff raise another issue for us. *What happens to the children of crazymakers?*

Amy's earliest memory is hiding at the top of the stairs late at night, listening to her parents fighting in the living room. As the fights escalated, Max Littleton would get louder and louder. Often her mother, Laura, would back down after he reached a certain level of ferocity, but occasionally she held her ground. Then there was no predicting where the fight could go.

By the time she was six years old, Amy had learned how

terrible these battles could become. And once the fight was over, her mother always broke down. Laura's crying felt particularly painful for Amy. The little girl would finally crawl back down the hall and sneak into her bed. She would go back to sleep terrified of what Max might eventually do to her mother. Any attack on a young girl's mother is like an attack on her personally, because of gender identification.

Amy can remember many, many times when she drifted off to sleep as she prayed for God to protect her mother. Her childhood world was filled with apprehension and fear of what might happen to her family. If God didn't shield them, they might perish in the night. Little Amy felt as though the Littleton home was under a terrible shadow.

Trying to Heal the Wounds

Today Amy is a client in one of Dr. Paul Meier's clinics, where she is trying to sort out her emotional issues. A university student, Amy often awakens in the middle of the night with nightmares, sweating and filled with dread. An extremely attractive young woman, Amy finds herself retreating from any meaningful relationship with men. The emotional wounds from her childhood are deeper than Amy likes to admit.

During her early counseling Dr. Meier led Amy back into

the world of those early memories. He would often ask her to think out loud about what occurred when the past turned into such a dark place. Memories flooded out of Amy's mind, revealing another effect of her father's problems: how she had been forced to face her own struggles silently.

Amy remembered that Max attempted to be a good father. Unfortunately, Max's best attempts crashed. Even though the upheavals were over minor issues, the effect on Amy was major.

When Amy was five years old, Max came up with the idea of taking his daughter out on a "date" so they could really get to know each other. At the outset, Amy was excited about the possibilities and knew the time would be wonderful. Max asked where she'd like to go, and off they went to the nearest Dairy Queen.

Amy remembered her father telling her she could have anything she wanted. An avid devotee of hot fudge, Amy ordered a sundae and a tall Coke. Everything was perfect. Max talked to Amy in a soft, understanding voice, asking about her friends in the neighborhood. Her father seemed extremely interested in this sensitive little girl, and Amy was delighted. Then Amy reached for a napkin abruptly and knocked her Coke over. The brown drink ran in every direction and then over the edge of the table.

Max leaped to his feet. "Look at what you've done. You idiot! You've spilled your Coke all over the place."

His harsh words cut Amy to the core. One second he had been her deeply understanding father; the next second Max was hollering like a madman. People in the booths turned around and looked at him with consternation in their eyes.

One of the fast-food workers stopped and threw up her hands. "Oh my!" she chimed in. "The kid's spilled her drink. Let me get a rag."

"Hurry," Max warned. "This sticky mess is going everywhere."

Amy wanted to crawl under the table. She felt tears welling up in her eyes and wondered what was coming next. Maybe her father would whack her with his hand. The wonderful date had turned into a nightmare, and Amy was sure she wouldn't wake up. Even though the spill was only an accident, Max was a *very* angry man.

Amy had not told anyone about this incident until she entered therapy. Along with a thousand other similar episodes, she had carefully hidden her embarrassment from public view. Somewhere during her childhood, Amy learned it was forbidden to tell any secrets that put her father in a negative light. Max had subliminally instilled that idea into the entire family.

Her teachers never heard anything but the best accounts from Amy. They thought of her as an extremely well-behaved and highly motivated student who was a joy to have in the classroom. The truth behind the scene: Amy lived in an emotional world shrouded under a blanket of fear.

The Untold Truth

"The truth is," Amy said to Dr. Meier, "everyone in the family of a crazymaker is profoundly affected by this person's unpredictable behavior. My brother has struggled with the same fears I have. He knows how impossible it is to stay balanced when you feel like you are living on top of a time bomb that can explode any minute."

"And how has your brother, Jeff, been affected?" Dr. Meier asked.

"Jeff has a hard time figuring out who he wants to be," Amy reported. "Some of the time, he knows my father's behavior is deplorable, but at other moments he demonstrates the same insensitivity. Jeff's confused because he knows how badly my father has hurt my mother. On the other hand, Dad is the only role model Jeff knows."

Dr. Meier told Amy that children often identify with the more aggressive parent, becoming like him or her. Jeff's behavior was predictable.

Amy expressed how deeply confusing the family disorder could become, because children are both drawn and repelled by their parent's disruptive behavior. How do you sort out what you want to keep and what you must reject? Amy and Jeff had hard decisions to make.

The children knew how appealing Max Littleton could be. They had seen him be an intelligent, creative person. Max could also be humorous and "work a crowd" like a pro. However, when the doors were closed and the shades pulled, he had the capacity to go off like a fireworks display. In those dark moments, everyone ran for cover.

And worst of all, even though Max did not sexually violate his daughter, he constantly pushed Amy's boundaries and made her feel apprehensive. It wasn't anything that he did physically, but she felt that her father looked at her in suggestive ways and treated her like a substitute wife instead of a daughter. He often made comments about how "sexy" she looked, and made other off-color remarks to her. After Amy went to college, Max wrote her letters, saying destructive things about her mother. Amy not only didn't need to hear such negativity, but she knew enough from the past not to trust her father's accounts. He was trying to brainwash her, and Amy resented the attempt.

Finally, Amy took the letters to Dr. Meier. After examining the issues, Dr. Meier helped see that these highly inflammatory letters were actually a form of "emotional incest." Emotional incest occurs when a parent treats an opposite-sex child like a substitute mate on an emotional and verbal level, but no physical sexual harassment occurs.

Sometimes, for example, a young divorced mother will continue to sleep in the same bed with her son until he is an older child or even a young teenager. She also might make him her "best friend" and her primary source of emotional support, instead of encouraging his peer relationships. This is also emotional incest and can have the same devastating emotional consequences as actual sexual incest.

About one in twenty females in America have had actual sexual intercourse with their fathers or stepfathers, and one in fifty men with their mothers or stepmothers. The incidence of emotional incest is significantly higher. Dr. Meier explained "emotional incest" to Amy. At this point, Amy began to realize how serious her father's problems were . . . and how deeply they were affecting her. Most people are naturally attracted to persons who are similar to their parent of the opposite sex, even when the parent has been a crazymaker. This tendency frightened Amy into avoiding all men.

Amy's father was truly a narcissistic crazymaker!

Facing the Results

Dr. Meier began helping Amy Littleton sort out her struggles and discover how the tentacles of fear of her father had reached into the corners of her mind. What areas had been affected and distorted by years of difficulty? Amy identified her most pressing problems.

First, Amy Littleton carried a latent fear of men, deeply distrusting the opposite sex. She worried about falling in love with a guy and then discovering he was her father all over again. Her apprehensions were not sexual as much as they were an overall suspicion of males. She had sensed her father would switch from one side of his personality to the other in an instant. While she wasn't equipped to recognize the personality dynamics in Max's behavior, Amy felt her father was more than a highly deceptive person. Because men were obviously physically stronger, Amy felt she had to be careful of having the strong arm placed on her. Consequently, Amy kept herself from getting too close to *any* man.

Second, Dr. Meier sensed the gender issue would probably spin off in another problem. Amy had grown up in the church and been faithful in her attendance, but Dr. Meier kept pushing. Was it possible Amy had any difficulties in relating to God?

When the crazymaker who dominated us is male, it is easy to think of the Creator in the same way as we may feel about men in general. While God is beyond gender, the masculine gender is usually used when speaking of Him. Amy soon realized she had difficulty in this area.

Believing in God wasn't the issue. Amy had grown up with a personal faith that made it almost impossible not to believe in the heavenly Father. However, no matter what she learned at church or in Bible studies, Amy found it difficult to feel close to the Almighty, and she was frightened of Him in an unhealthy way. It would take some work to pull this problem apart.

The Littleton family battles had created a split in how Amy saw God. On one side, she intellectually knew God was her friend. Amy had memorized many Scripture passages that assured her of His devotion and constant care. She could philosophize about how caring He had to be. But on the other hand, Amy felt something different. On the level of her emotions, God seemed like the enemy. Her many nights of hiding at the top of the stairs had contaminated Amy's perspective. When Amy prayed her bedtime prayers as a child, she was unconsciously thinking, *Dear heavenly version of my earthly father.*

As she talked about these confusing factors, Amy came to see an extremely important fact. Her father, Max, *wasn't* God Almighty! Often parents seem to have an omnipotence that borders on divinity, but Amy knew such an idea was a fantasy. Recognizing the distortion in her feelings was the start of getting her religious ideas in the right order. Amy went back to the Bible and began to rethink a number of important passages.

One passage from Psalms 119 particularly touched her. "Your faithfulness endures to all generations" (v. 90). The

Scriptures promised Amy that God was a dependable source of strength and guidance. She could push her feelings aside and trust Him. Amy knew she had to change how she felt about God . . . and men!

"Dear God," she prayed in Dr. Meier's office, "please help me to get to know You as You really are, and forgive me for thinking I was so angry with You when I was actually so angry and fearful of my father."

A Message for Other Children

After hours of working to get her mind and emotions back in the order they should be, Amy had a word for children of difficult parents: *Your relationships at home will affect every other relationship in your life!*

Growing up in the midst of controversy and confusion is difficult, but not as hard as trying to act as if the problems did not exist. You can't hide your fears, believing in time they will work themselves out. They don't! Negative emotions have to be identified, explored, and resolved. They don't blow away.

In addition, the patterns we see in our parents slip under our skin and become the masks we wear. Amy knew her brother, Jeff, had picked up many of his father's habits and was developing a tendency to be an explosive person. Negative behavior can be absorbed as easily as it can be rejected. As we move into our adult years, it is necessary to return to the past and examine how we developed our responses. If we have grown up in a world of crazymakers, we will have patterns that must be modified.

One of the most significant habits we must break is the tendency to harbor everything that happens until we have built up an enormous bubble of silence around ourselves, like immune-deficient children who are sealed in a plastic bubble to protect them. Max Littleton's image of perfection was one of those invisible barriers. Amy's path back to wholeness began when she burst the balloon.

You must recognize the importance of talking to a safe, secure mentor or a professional counselor or minister. That's where the door to a better future opens. Amy soon stopped demanding perfection from herself.

Here are several conclusions for you to write down and carry with you. Repeated attention to these issues will help children of crazymakers get free of their hang-ups.

1. *Break the bubble!* Recognize that your tendency to harbor family secrets is *destructive to you.* Make the decision that you will no longer tolerate this old pattern. You can't afford to carry the responsibility any further.

2. *Find a friend!* Everyone needs a confidant. Find a trustworthy source to be the repository of your past. You may

have to do some searching, but start looking for a caring, listening person who will stand with you, regardless of what happens.

3. *Our parents aren't God; God isn't our parents!* Check out how your relationship with the Almighty functions. Any anger and reservation you have today probably came out of yesterday. Now is the time to let go of the past and start living in the present by putting your parents in the right place.

Here's the message Amy lives by today. "This I recall to my mind, Therefore I have hope. The LORD's lovingkindness indeed never cease, For His compassions never fail. They are new every morning. Great is Thy faithfulness" (Lam. 3:21–23 NASB). Rather than let old memories contaminate her, Amy now trusts God to direct her path by His faithfulness.

She has found that every day is a new day!

chapterNINE

Maintaining Stability

We have met an interesting group of friends. From Jack and Ann Smith to George and Sally Harris and through their families to other assorted friends, we've watched crazy-making at work. We have encountered both difficult people and full-blown narcissists. They are certainly not an easy crowd to run with!

Remember we created the word *crazymaker* to paint a picture of how these people *affect us*. The point of this book is to discover new ways to respond when damaging people's big guns are aimed at our heads. While we cannot change anyone, we are able to alter ourselves and avoid getting blown apart by people who lack empathy.

In this chapter we want to take a further in-depth look at what makes crazymakers "tick" and see if increased insight will help us find new ways to deal with individuals who are endeavoring to dominate us. Let's explore a few other issues concerning their personality needs.

Meet Manager Mary

Mary Jones, the owner and manager of a children's clothing store, held staff discussions each week, during which her five employees were encouraged to be candid and forthright. Unfortunately, Mary didn't like something Judy Jackson had said during a discussion. An hour after the staff meeting, Mary cornered Judy in her office.

"Judy," Mary said with a big smile across her face, "I need to ask you a question."

"Sure," Judy answered, shuffling her papers together.

"During the staff meeting, I noticed that you didn't like the way I staged our storefront windows this week . . . the area where the public does most of their window shopping." Mary kept her contrived grin locked in place.

"Yes." Judy nodded her head. "I thought your last display looked regal, expensive, high dollar. You know . . . a level of expense that might discourage our customers."

"Our customers?" Mary kept smiling. "Are you suggesting that we should lower our standards?"

Judy shrugged. "I thought we might price ourselves out of our market if we look like we're out of the reach of the young working couples in their twenties. That's all. Most of our customers are working-class people."

"*Working-class people!*" Mary's smile faded quickly. "Well, I never thought of us as trying to sweep the Wal-Mart crowd in here."

Judy laughed. "Wal-Mart? Hey, that's where the money is."

"Listen, Judy." Mary abruptly stuck her finger in her assistant's face. "I'm aiming at the country-club crowd. I don't want anyone thinking I'm one of those floor-scrubbing types. Got me?"

Judy raised her eyebrows and blinked in surprise. "I thought our job was to make money."

"Your job is to do what I tell you," Mary snapped. "The quality of the people I serve is more important than making a quick dime. Start deciding how we get in touch with *my* sort of folks." Mary stomped out of the room.

Judy stared with her mouth hanging open. Although they had never talked about it, Judy knew Mary Jones had grown up in a small town *in a working-class family*. Mary had very little money when she started her clothing business. Who was she kidding? Why the personal attack?

The Big Front

Mary and Judy's conversation displays one of the key ingredients in what makes difficult people who they are. *Mary was more concerned with how she appeared publicly than how she felt privately.* This sort of crazymaker turns on a fixed point; she projects an image that is more important than anything else to her. In fact, Mary would even deny her own emotions when her feelings contradicted this image.

During her childhood, Mary was taught that she must not display the depth of the anger she often felt. "Wealthy people don't get mad," her mother advised Mary, "so we shouldn't either." Today when Mary starts to develop wrath, she will keep smiling and repress her rage. No one ever sees the depth of her animosity. Manager Mary's interest was keeping her cherished image in place regardless of how the conversation impacted Judy.

Image is *everything* to a crazymaker!

As Allan Cole's employees and Amy Littleton discovered, it's critical for difficult people to maintain the right image. While Allan Cole and Max Littleton wouldn't have recognized this, they were oblivious to many of the values that motivate most people. Characteristics such as integrity, self-expression, and personal dignity were not a part of their thinking. Rather, they constantly thought about self-promotion to further establish that all-important self-image they were busily maintaining.

Another way to state crazymakers' problem: they lack a true sense of themselves. In their childhood development, they didn't form the internal goals that can lead well-balanced people toward a meaningful life. Instead, a foreboding sense of emptiness formed at the center of their being.

What Do We Learn?

When we encounter anyone from a difficult person, like Mary Jones, to a narcissist, like Ann Smith, we need to step back and ask ourselves several questions. Let's ponder some of the key issues.

1. What image is this person trying to project? For example, the morning after their confrontation, Judy had this conversation with Manager Mary.

"Mary, I've been thinking about what you said last night. Maybe I've missed an important ingredient in what you want to accomplish with this store. Can you tell me about your dreams for this business?"

Mary thought for a moment and then smiled her usual artificial grin. "I want the world to know Mary Jones runs an exquisite children's store where the best people shop." She straightened slightly. "I intend for top-rung people to do their shopping here."

Judy nodded her head. "Maybe, we ought to talk about that goal in our next meeting."

"Yes!" Mary beamed. "I'll tell anyone this is my goal."

Judy realized the sudden resistance from Mary the evening before indicated something was cooking in the back room that had never been laid on the table. She sensed Mary lacked a solid perception of herself; her storefront display was actually promoting who Mary wanted to be: the prestigious owner of an elite children's shop. Manager Mary was promoting Manager Mary.

When you are mystified about a personal attack, and you are trying to assemble the broken pieces in the puzzle, take a new approach. Is it possible that the difficult person might *actually* be concerned with the inner self-concept he or she projects? Think the possibility over. It may help defuse the bomb.

2. What values is this person ready to toss? Jack Smith wanted a good marriage, but Ann's interest was in dominating him. She was willing to jettison a meaningful relationship to achieve her goal. Sally Harris desired a happy family, but George was set on making a good impression on the community. When all the cards were played, Allan Cole only wanted production and didn't care what employees thought of him. Each person was willing to discard something in order to get what he or she wanted (but none would dare name it out loud).

See how it works?

When people are willing to dispense with core human values, their behavior becomes mechanical and they function like automatons. Difficult people make you feel as though you are arguing with a talking machine, grinding away at some abstract goal you don't understand. Unfortunately, no one can have a personal relationship with a gearbox.

You need to listen carefully as the gears in a difficult person's mind grind together. Try to identify what this person has lost from his or her value system. For instance, he may suppress acts of kindness or lose all sense of other individuals' need to be important. Often you can appeal to that dimension of human values, and then be able to help the crazymaker get in touch with his or her best self. You may have to sneak up on their blind side, but the attempt is worth the effort.

One evening as they were closing the clothing store, Judy turned around and spoke to Mary. "You work so hard," Judy said. "Don't you ever get tired?"

"Sure," Mary said with her usual indifference. "But at least I sleep at night."

"What do you do for fun?" Judy asked. "For relaxation?"

Mary looked blank for a moment. "I guess . . . my store is my fun."

Judy kept the pleasant look on her face, but pushed. "Wouldn't it be great to find something that was more important than selling clothes to rich people?"

A puzzled countenance flashed across Mary's face.

"You can't put children's clothes in your casket," Judy said bluntly. "You need to find out what gives you lasting joy." Judy took Mary's hand. "Think about it." When Judy left the store, Mary was still standing in the office with a perplexed look on her face.

The recovery of values can soften the toughest person. Like Judy, when we put a difficult person back in touch with enduring dreams and hopes, we have a good chance of creating change.

3. *How do we stay balanced?* Perhaps the word *crazymaker* is more appropriate than we might have first thought. Think about the application of the word *crazy* to the difficult people in your life. When a person's self-image is more important than being loved, doesn't that suggest an individual is at least somewhat on the crazy side? After all, this person is denying the most fundamental human need to obtain a fairly meaningless goal.

Actually people like Ann Smith, George Harris, and Allan Cole can seem insane when they are expressing full-blown anger. They are completely out of touch with what is good, true, meaningful, and genuinely human. As we say on the street, they have "flipped out." And their behavior has a similar effect *on us.*

In order to stay stable, we need to gain some distance from the conversation. At least in our own minds, we must find an objective place to stand where we can regain or maintain our perspective.

We need to give ourselves "reminders." For example, when a crazymaker attacks, we should have a number of sentences stored away in our memory that we can call forth to keep the context of the confrontation clear in our minds. Here are some examples of reminders that can help.

FACTS TO REMEMBER

To keep yourself balanced, ask yourself questions like:

- *Is this person stable?*
- *Is he or she making sense, or is this actually a distortion?*
- *Why is he or she acting so crazy?*

It also helps to have introspective reminders like:

- *I am not crazy.*
- *I am not going crazy.*
- *I refuse to accept this assault as valid.*

When a harsh person is hitting us with hurricane force, and we feel as though we're just about to go sliding into a brick building, we need to stop and bring one of these "reminders" to mind. For a few moments, this will create a mental distance from the collision. Even though the time may be short, it will give us the space we need to recover our equilibrium.

The first few times you attempt to use these "reminders," they may feel awkward, but don't stop. Keep trying. This internal process will keep you from thinking you are on the crazy side. That's not an insignificant goal!

The Bottom Line

When we go back and survey the families we have looked at so far, one conclusion can't be escaped: each of these harsh individuals attacked without empathy. Difficult individuals are so absorbed in their own concerns that they don't "feel" with other people.

Our task is to try and put crazymakers back in touch with their most human feelings. The job isn't easy, but it is worth everything it costs. The world of literature is filled with the stories of the change in personality that follow after people get back in touch with gentleness, joy, pain, and meaning.

Every Christmas, multitudes wait for the story of Ebenezer Scrooge to appear on television. His change from a penny-pinching, indifferent creditor to the kindly godfather of Tiny Tim is a tale of a man's transformation from narcissist to philanthropist. Each year we listen to this story of radical change as the hard heart of this mean man is warmed by the kindest and most sensitive of human values.

Jesus had a similar effect on Zacchaeus. The hard-nosed chief tax collector was hated not only because he was an agent of Rome, but also because he extorted from his own people to make himself rich. The story in Luke 19 tells us that Zacchaeus was small in size. We can surmise he made himself "big" by forcing people to buckle under to him. There's a picture of a crazymaker.

Rather than attack this defiled, sinful man, Jesus came to his house for supper. As was the custom of the ancient world, Jesus' actions proclaimed to the public that he was a close friend of Zacchaeus. The little man was profoundly touched by the big thing Jesus had done. Jesus affirmed an individual everyone else wanted to kill.

The difference?

The story ends with Zacchaeus shouting from the rooftop that he will give away half of his riches to the poor and repay anyone he had extorted four times the amount he took. Zacchaeus and Scrooge could go down the road arm in arm as renewed human beings!

Evoking the presence of Jesus is the transforming act with the power to change the cold-hearted into loving people. Because the love of Jesus is so powerful, it can do what none of us can accomplish by ourselves! Let's see how we make this commitment by returning to the story of Zacchaeus. We need to do exactly what he did.

First, Jesus made it clear that He wanted to go to Zacchaeus's house, which meant that Zacchaeus had to change his perspective and the way he dealt with people. The Scripture makes it evident that Jesus wanted to be a part of Zacchaeus's life. In the same way that this little man in Jericho invited the Lord Jesus in, you need to clearly ask Jesus to be a part of everything happening in your life. Of course, this means a willingness to change how you see things and deal with people. Zacchaeus went home and turned his house upside down, cleaning, improving, and preparing to welcome the Lord. We need to do the same thing, getting rid of anything that might prove offensive to Jesus. Look carefully at what you keep in those secret closets in the back of your mind. Invite Jesus to be part of *everything that happens* to you.

Asking the Lord Jesus to be part of your life is also inviting Him to stand with you in your struggle with a crazymaker. You can expect Him to stand beside you the next time a confrontation starts. While you will not be able to see Him, Jesus is there, waiting to help you. The next time one of the explosions occurs, remind yourself that the Prince of Peace is standing by your side. You have a friend walking with you in the battle.

Second, Zacchaeus opened his heart. He was prepared to become a righteous person. When Zacchaeus told Jesus that he would give back the money he had taken from others, the little man was making a big decision. He was reaching into the center of his life where money had become God. Zacchaeus pushed financial accumulation aside and responded with the same love he had experienced in Jesus, the great giver. Perhaps, your area of concern is not money, but regardless of what it is, you need to open your heart to be a person of goodwill, hope, and honest response. How could you reach out to help meet the needs of others? Think about it carefully because this is part of evoking the presence of Jesus.

And this means you are willing to help meet the needs of the difficult person or narcissist. However, you are not agreeing to meet their illegitimate needs. As you will discover throughout this book, crazymakers have problems they do not recognize. You might be able to help them in unraveling these problems. While you may feel hostile toward these people, you can still pray for a change of heart, just as Zacchaeus did for himself.

Third, Zacchaeus surrendered to the love of Jesus. Where vengeance had invaded his world and taken his best dreams captive, the tax collector refused to harbor ill will any longer. Rather, he would treat the people around him with the same concern Jesus had given him. We are not suggesting you become a doormat or a less-resilient person. Quite the contrary! However, it's not easy to feel kindly toward the crazymakers in our world. They have unleashed so much difficulty on us that we may want them smashed, broken, and vanquished. Unfortunately, retaliation leads to more confrontation. Only the love of Jesus can reverse the course taken by thoughts of revenge. As our lives are changed by His love, possibilities of renewal are opened up for the self-absorbed people we must confront.

Love can be warm and gentle as well as firm and persistent. Many of us are capable of loving people who are obviously broken and hurting. It's another story when we are confronting the insensitive and callous. Regardless of the target, nothing prepares us for the battle like a heart filled with the love of Jesus. Our minds and our emotions become focused. We are able to cut through the smoke and see the truth about the issues. While it may not seem possible, it is still true that the love of Jesus can change people who would otherwise be untouchable.

Don't hesitate to invite the power of Jesus into all of these problems. His love is the key to positive change!

Moving On

In the next section of the book, we will examine six steps that can help you help your crazymaker seek revision of his or her behavior. We will suggest specific procedures designed to bring change. No matter how demanding the struggles have been with a crazymaker, don't give up. You can get along with that difficult person in your life!

partTWO

GETTING THE "CRAZY" OUT: SIX STEPS OUT OF YOUR CRISIS

chapter TEN

Step One: Identify the History of the Problem

Every personal confrontation has a history. Getting in touch with the past is one way to begin changing the future. We need to remember the what, when, where, how, and why that made the collision occur. Remembering is vital to correction.

Our first step out of the chaos is to identify the history of the problem.

Jack Smith and Sally Harris shared a similar problem. While what happened in their families was quite different, these victims of crazymaking started out at the same place. They were convinced the family problems *began with them.*

They were certain that something in their pasts, their reactions, their habits had created the explosive environment. This sense of certainty operated like blinders.

In Jack's case, he was sure that a communication problem had developed between him and Ann. His answer to their collisions was to keep talking. Saying it "one more time" would make everything clear. Of course, Ann was eating him alive while Jack kept buzzing.

While Sally wouldn't have said so out loud, her problem was her innate assumption that she was always wrong. George simply seemed to be strong, powerful, a driver's-seat type of guy. How could he be wrong? No question about it! The trouble was Sally. Right?

Wrong!

Both Jack and Sally felt as if they were trapped in a labyrinth, going around in circles and getting nowhere. When they sought counseling, both were actually seeking clarification on what they were certain was wrong with them.

Seeking the Long-Distance View

Drs. Meier and Wise have both discovered from their counseling practices that most people living with a crazymaker have a similar starting point: they assume something about themselves that isn't correct. They overcome this by recovering a long-distance view of their entire situation, including the difficult person's perspective.

After living or working with a difficult person for a period of time, spouses or employees generally settle into the mode of denying the actual problem is happening *to them*. They accept the daily routine of confrontation as a "normal" family or business life. After all, isn't everybody this way? If the crazymaker is skillful enough, the victim starts to accept the difficult person as more intelligent and keeps giving in to this perceived superior intelligence. Often children grow up in homes where shouting and accusing is an everyday event. The kids develop the expectation that more of the same will follow with someone they haven't yet met. Does any of this sound vaguely familiar to you? If it does, it's time to develop a larger and broader perspective.

Sound footing out of the maze requires you to recognize the truth about your personal situation immediately!

Waking Up!

One night prior to the backyard explosion in the Harris home, George Harris grew particularly angry with thirteen-year-old Andrew. The boy had slightly stretched the truth about an incident at school, which is not uncommon for a teenager.

"I want to know *exactly* what occurred." George pushed Andrew up against the wall. "Tell me."

"I told you," Andrew mumbled.

Suddenly George slapped his son. "Don't lie to me," George demanded. "I've already talked to your teacher."

Andrew's mouth dropped, and he started crying. "I just talked once too often when I should have been listening to the teacher."

"Once?" George's voice became louder. "The truth is you are a constant disruption in the classroom."

"No," Andrew protested weakly. "I shouldn't have tried to talk to my friend when the teacher was teaching."

George pushed Andrew harder. "The truth is you are on your way to becoming a juvenile delinquent. You never tell the truth. If you don't straighten up, I'll take a belt to you every time you get out of line."

Sally was listening in the kitchen and didn't know what to do. She didn't want to undercut her husband's authority, but George was turning a splinter into major surgery. Actually Andrew was quite truthful.

As Sally considered the problem, she knew Andrew needed discipline, but the transgression seemed a normal problem for a boy his age. *Something* was wrong with her husband. And she needed more insight.

Sally's challenge was sorting out what was wrong in her thinking. She had assumed that whatever George did with the children was acceptable, but it wasn't. He said harmful things that could have a destructive effect on their son. In addition, she couldn't be wrong in this situation, as she always assumed, since she was not part of this argument. She needed to go back to the beginning and sort out what had been missed. Sally was waking up.

Start Evaluating Yourself

When a new client arrives at one of Paul Meier's clinics, the person enters the counseling process by going through an intake process. A staff member sits down with the client and asks questions, covering the full range of where the patient has come from, where the person is now, and where he or she hopes to go. The clinician will ask thought-provoking questions to help open the person's eyes to dimensions of his or her problems. The questionnaires are detailed and raise new possibilities, helping each person get in touch with what is happening in his or her life. Inevitably, discovering the individual's history is the start of finding his or her way out of the emotional maze.

You can do the same thing. While you probably don't have the background to develop the questions that a clinician would ask, you can begin to work your way out of the wilderness you have been living in. Based on questionnaires used in the Meier Clinics, the following is a series of prompts and questions that can lead you into a new understanding of yourself. Remember as you compose your answers that you want to know everything you possibly can about why you act and react as you do.

Meet the Inner You!

Describe where you live and whether you are married, single, or divorced.

_____

_____

_____

Describe your mate and his or her job. What are your feelings about your spouse at this time?

_____

_____

_____

Describe yourself. Where were you born and when?

_____

_____

_____

_____

Describe your father and his profession.

_____

_____

_____

Describe how your father treated you during the first six years of your life.

_____

_____

_____

Describe any time your father became emotionally, physically, or sexually abusive toward you. Toward your siblings. Toward your mom. Toward anyone.

_____

_____

_____

Describe what you like about your dad.

_____

_____

_____

Describe anything you wish you could change about the way your father treated you.

_____

_____

_____

Look at yourself through your dad's eyes. What do you see?

_____

_____

_____

Describe how the real you differs from the "you" your father perceives.

_____

_____

_____

Describe the emotions you usually felt toward your father while growing up.

_____

_____

_____

Is your father still alive? If not, when and how did he die?

_____

_____

_____

Describe any fantasies about his future relationship with you that ended when he died.

_____

_____

_____

When you picked male friends throughout your life, did you tend to pick guys who were like your father? Why do you think you made those choices?

_____

_____

_____

Is it possible that these choices were a way to fill a hole in your soul because you were never as emotionally close to your dad as you wish you could have been? Or is it possible that these choices in your relationships with males were an attempt to "fix" your father? Describe any ways you tried to "fix" these male friends.

_____

_____

_____

Did you ever unconsciously attempt to get vengeance on your father by getting into vengeful relationships with these "father substitutes"? How so?

_____

_____

_____

Describe negative things you say to yourself when you make mistakes.

_____

_____

_____

Would you say those same negative things to your best friends? Why or why not?

_____

_____

_____

Why do you say these things to yourself? Did any of these messages come from statements your father made to or about you?

_____

_____

_____

After you have thought about these last two questions long enough to fully answer, we want you to consider taking another step. Could you take your Bible and write inside the cover a statement that today you decide to become your *own* best friend, recording today's date? You will attempt to never again say negative things to yourself that you wouldn't say to your very best friend. If you are willing to make this decision, put this book down. Get your Bible and write this inside the cover and date it and sign it.

Now that you have considered this step, let's explore those negative messages you carry with you a little further.

Did your father imply any of these negative messages to you without actually saying them? Maybe he gave you nonverbal messages, such as implying you should not bother him when he is busy. Was he reading the sports page, but you felt he was really trying to avoid the emotional crisis you were in at that moment? What do you remember?

_____

_____

_____

What other "don't exist" messages did he give you verbally or nonverbally?

_____

_____

When you think about these issues from the past, do you feel like dying? If your answer is yes, take a deep breath and let yourself relax as you think about this very difficult question. Do not push yourself beyond what you can deal with.

_____

_____

_____

Is it possible that any death wish you might have today is the result of how you felt during childhood? Describe any childhood events during which you felt like a nuisance or that people would be better off if you were not around?"

_____

_____

_____

Did you feel unconditionally loved by your father or did you feel that you had to earn his love? Describe this.

_____

_____

_____

Do you still base your self-worth on what your father thought of you in the past or thinks of you now?

_____

_____

_____

Since six billion people live on planet Earth and your father is only one of them, can you see how fruitless it is to base your opinion of yourself on one person's opinion?

_____

_____

_____

If Jesus had been your father's child instead of you, would your father still have been abusive and critical? (Sound obvious? Maybe, it's not. Give it some careful analysis.)

_____

_____

_____

By this time, you've probably begun to sense that your father had his own set of problems that had nothing to do with you. Some of your pain may have grown out of your father's inner contradictions and inconsistencies. The truth is that it wasn't your fault that your father wasn't closer to you than he was. You can count on that fact!

As you've been answering these prompts and questions, it may have occurred to you that the issue wasn't really with your father as much as it was with your mother. (Or maybe you had problems with both of your parents.) Possibly your mother was the source of many of your struggles. Please go back now and do this section over again, using *her* name instead of your father's.

In counseling sessions, as clients attempt to answer some of the above prompts and questions, many will cry. Please don't feel strange or out of order if you find yourself weeping as you deal with some issues. Many of the ways we struggle with difficult people are conditioned by how we related to our parents. Eighty-five percent of your adult personality was formed during the first six years of your life. Therefore, as adults, our expectations of how other people will respond to us is related to conditioning in our childhoods. You many find yourself making important discoveries about your life today.

What About the Other Kids?

Now, that we've looked at your parents, let's turn our attention to the rest of your family. How many brothers and sisters or stepsiblings were in your family?

_____

_____

_____

Describe your role in your family of origin. Are you the first-born, middle child, or the youngest? In this role how did you interact with the rest of the family?

_____

_____

_____

Is it possible you were the substitute parent and ended up being robbed of some of your childhood? (Think back to the interaction in your family and consider your answer carefully.)

_____

_____

_____

Were you ever a scapegoat?

_____

_____

_____

Were you ever treated like a substitute mate for the parent of the opposite sex . . . ?

_____

_____

_____

Did it ever occur to you that being a substitute parent is called "emotional incest" and can have terrible effects on you (see page 106)?

_____

_____

_____

Many people are as strongly affected by their brothers and sisters as they are by their parents. You may have formed many of your expectations from one of these people and are still acting and reacting out of those original encounters. Spend plenty of time recalling how those relationships worked for you, and if one seems particularly troublesome, go back and repeat the prompts and questions for this sibling.

After you have considered the foregoing assignment, let's turn our attention to a different direction.

What About God?

Do you have a personal relationship with God?

_____

_____

_____

Describe how this experience began and how it is occurring today.

_____

_____

_____

What do you think God is like?

_____

_____

_____

What might He be thinking *about you* right now?

_____

_____

_____

How close is your description of God to what you said about your father or mother or sibling? (Possibly your answer feels a little astonishing.)

_____

_____

_____

Is it possible you could be confusing the loving God of the Bible with your own projections of your father or mother? (Ponder that for a while.)

As you were saying your bedtime prayers as a child, could you have been thinking, *Dear heavenly version of my earthly father (or mother or sibling)?* If so, before you record your answer, you need to stop right now and pray a different prayer. Would you be willing to say, "Dear God, whoever You really are, will You make Yourself known to me and help me during this time in my life?"

Ask yourself if this is exactly what you need to pray right now. If so, please put this book down and ask God to make Himself known to you as He truly is. Spend a few minutes asking God to become an important part of your life.

We hope these past few minutes have been a productive time for you. Developing a personal relationship with the real God who designed you will help you find new strength and guidance in your struggles with the difficult people in your life.

Now let's turn your attention in a different direction and consider some of the destructive ways in which your life may have been affected in the past. Consider the negative events that have happened to you.

What About the Negative Situations in Your Past?

Were you ever emotionally, physically, or sexually abused by anyone in your life?

_____

_____

_____

If yes, please give a brief history of everyone who ever abused you in any way. (Describe this out loud, right now if possible. Let yourself hear your own words detailing what happened to you in the past.)

_____

_____

_____

If you've had one or more of these terrible experiences, did you feel unprotected by a parent or God or by anyone else during those times?

_____

_____

_____

Do you realize that the parent who knowingly allows you to be abused is just as abusive as the person who hurt you? How does that make you feel right now? (Describe your feelings out loud if possible.)

_____

_____

_____

You do not have to believe those negative messages about your worth. This is the moment to accept the real truth about yourself. You are not a "human doing," but a "human being." You are of *infinite worth and deserve to be loved. You deserve to be loved by people who know all of your secrets.*

At this moment you might want to open your Bible and read Psalm 139. You will discover that God was thinking about you last night as you fell asleep as well as this morning as you woke up. He is thinking about you so many times today, you can't even count them. From the moment you were conceived in your mother's womb, the loving hand of

God has been upon you. You may find these facts to be hard to believe, but they are true!

Maybe, you've been mad at God for not protecting you better. Even as counselors, we can become angry with God when we hear stories like yours. We don't really know why He allows so much abuse to happen in this fallen world, but we have faith that someday in heaven, He will give us a reasonable explanation. We do know that harboring vengeful motives only makes us more depressed, and no difficult person or narcissist is worth being depressed over. All we can do is to turn our own vengeful feelings over to God and protect ourselves from further abuse. Possibly you would like to do that right now. Let's change direction and look in another area. Let's look at your emotional history.

A Look at Your Emotional History

When you were growing up, did you often feel more depressed than your friends?

_____

_____

_____

Did depression ever exist in your immediate family? (If so, mention the person or persons in the space below and describe their type or types of depression.)

_____

_____

_____

Do you have other relatives who struggled with depression, anxiety, or other mental problems? If so, describe this in the space below.

_____

_____

_____

Could your depression be genetic? Due to circumstances? Or both?

_____

_____

_____

Have you ever felt so depressed you wished you could die?

_____

_____

_____

Have you ever attempted suicide or come close to it? When?

_____

_____

_____

What strengths did you draw on to keep from doing this?

_____

_____

_____

Stop for a moment and recognize an important fact. Maybe you're one of those people who have seriously thought about suicide. You may feel that you are alive today only because you were too "chicken" to carry it out. Well, that's simply not true. You are alive today because you possess strengths such as bravery and hope. You were courageous enough to keep yourself alive in the middle of your horrible pain. You can rejoice in who you are! Why not do so right now? Give yourself a big pat on the back!

Let's take a more intense look at depression. You could be struggling with another type of problem.

How many times in your life have you experienced a major depression lasting a month or longer when you felt bad enough that you wanted to die?

_____

_____

_____

Did these depressions come out of nowhere and exist in a regular pattern? Or did they occur after a rejection or during a crisis period? Describe the circumstances.

_____

_____

_____

On the other hand, is it possible you could have had a physical problem, like inheriting a low serotonin level or a low thyroid hormone level, both of which can cause suicidal depression?

_____

_____

_____

When was the last time you felt happy and peaceful for several months in a row?

_____

_____

_____

Do you ever feel too happy for two or more days in a row, talking faster and dominating conversations? During these times do you sleep less, have racing thoughts, and blow money on credit-card spending? Do you flirt more, get creative ideas, become grandiose, or have to keep moving because you can't sit still?

_____

_____

_____

Many people have inherited bipolar disorders that will create these symptoms described in the questions above. If your answers fit such a possibility, you will want to talk with a psychiatrist who can put a halt to these mood swings with a mood-stabilizing medication *and* an antidepressant. (An antidepressant all by itself can make bipolar *worse*. Both medications are needed together in people with *bipolar* mood swings.)

Have you ever felt for no good reason that your telephones were bugged or someone might poison you? Have you ever had a tendency to become paranoid, thinking strangers are saying negative things about you?

_____

_____

_____

The fears indicated in the questions above are also signs that a psychiatrist is necessary to give you a dopamine-correcting medication that will make the paranoia disappear, usually within a few days. The longer a person stays paranoid and off medications, the harder it becomes to have total recovery.

Have you ever developed lifelong patterns of counting things when you enter a room? Checking the doors three times a night instead of once? Washing your hands thirty times a day? Do you starve yourself to an unsafe weight or vomit compulsively for weight control?

_____

_____

_____

It's possible that repetitious activities are a clue that you are dealing with obsessive-compulsive patterns to avoid getting in touch with feelings. These are certainly treatable traits. Again, you should consult a counselor or psychiatrist. Serotonin medications make these habits disappear within a month or two. Some people with Obsessive Compulsive Disorder (OCD) can recover with therapy alone, but many will never recover without higher doses of serotonin medications.

We have covered a number of very important areas to help you get in touch with yourself. If you've been able to answer these questions in a forthright manner, you should know yourself much better.

In addition, you may have gained some sense of what has happened in the past. If the difficult person or narcissist in your life seems open to this same kind of review, ask that person to also go through this experience.

Now, what will you do with this data? In order to develop a method of examining your experience so you can discover new insights, try the following process that can help you open closed doors. The process is called journaling.

The Process of Journaling

Developing a journal is an important way to keep in touch with your thoughts and feelings. Often people use a journal to write down their problems as they attempt to work out the details of what has happened to them. Many times keeping a journal will help clarify an issue we haven't been able to understand. Moreover, a journal can help us write out our personal history in a form we can analyze and begin to see in a new light. Be sure to write down your *emotions* as well as historical facts.

When Sally started trying to understand what had occurred between her husband and her son, she needed to get the big picture into focus. Like bringing the focus on a camera into clarity, the picture of her relationship with George and Andrew had to be much more finely tuned. Journaling did that for her. Not only could she write out what had occurred, but also Sally was able to read a description of the events again and again in her own words. Each time she read the journal, her grasp of the problem became clearer and more complete.

HOW TO KEEP TRACK OF YOURSELF

First, either find or buy a book filled with blank pages. Sometimes diaries are published that are numbered for each day of the year. By writing on the date listed in the diary you have a permanent way of remembering when situations happened on a day-by-day basis. Other diaries are filled with only empty pages. Choose what works best for you.

Second, think *exactly* about what you need to record. Often, people will write down events and then on the following pages dissect the meaning. For example, Sally could have described how George manhandled Andrew before trying to understand what was going on in the encounter. After finishing her journaling, she might have left some space for other notations as later reflections developed, such as whether she is being protective enough of her children as motherhood demands, or if she is allowing her own selfishness, fear, or desire for financial security to influence her to look the other way.

Often, a person will write what he or she is thinking about, describing in detail what is running through his mind at that moment. One thought will lead to another thought. As each idea is recorded, material is provided for insight. By the time the journaler has come to the end of a section, a totally new and different scenario will have presented itself.

While we are not able to accurately describe how all of the people involved in a particular event saw what happened, we can come to our own firm conclusion about what it meant to us. That's the real goal of journaling.

Remember when we first met Sally Brown Harris? At the evening supper table, she had asked her husband, George, if he had replaced their worn tires. The question provoked a frightening exchange that left Sally in tears. George accused her of trying to run all of their lives by remote control.

If Sally had chosen to journal about this problem, she might have written out the details of who said what to whom. Then, Sally could have started analyzing the meaning of what occurred. She would have quickly recognized that George attacked her because she had revealed his mistake: he forgot to purchase crucial items. Sally might have come to see that George became defensive to protect himself from perceived criticism.

Remember. *The first step out of the chaos is to identify the history of the problem.*

Now, go back and reread your journal days later. Immediately after you write your thoughts, it is possible that nothing is clear. Give it more time. Often we have to live with an event a couple of days before it starts to make sense.

As we ponder some incident in the past, we may find that the problem becomes a bit like solving a mystery. Initially, we cannot understand who did what to whom, creating the crime. The clues are there, but we can't make the jagged pieces fit together. Then later, often abruptly, we will suddenly realize some insignificant event actually meant much more. At that moment our perspective changes and we see the situation in a completely different light.

Great pieces of literature have this character. As we read an intriguing story, the author leaves clues that do not seem to be particularly important. However, the longer we read, the more we understand how crucial the incident was. Only as we delve into the story does an insignificant event take on its true perspective. Then, the larger story clarifies itself.

Journaling helps us throw a spotlight on difficult behavior so we can put collisions in a long-range perspective. By considering what we have written later, we will begin to put each episode in proper order.

Finally, find a safe place to hide your journal. People often make a critical mistake of leaving this little book lying around. If it's sitting on a table, someone will pick up the journal and read it. Who's the most likely to take a peek? The person you're writing about. You can bet on it!

You cannot write fully and confidentially unless you have found a place to hide your diary where you know your heart's desires are safe and secure. If you are going to pour out your heart, the revelation demands a certainty that no one will be able to read your most personal thoughts. You must make sure the location is absolutely, totally, completely, uncompromisingly, certainly, and finally secure!

Our Goal

There are many reasons for journaling, but our task in this chapter is singular. The objective is to help you know yourself better and to identify the full history of your problem with a crazymaker. Your goal is to stay in touch with these two objectives. Who are you in your interaction with this person and why is this person attacking you? Figure it out.

Again, the first step out of the chaos is to identify the history of the problem.

chapter ELEVEN

Step Two:
Set Boundaries That Bring Change

While we have already mentioned boundaries, let's take a deeper, longer look at this topic. We have described two types of crazymakers: difficult individuals and narcissists. The scale escalates as crazymakers lose their ability to feel for other people. Their diminishing empathy produces increased insensitivity. Of course, that means *greater pain for you!*

As the problem of indifference worsens, it becomes increasingly important to create fences that protect you from these assaults. These walls will help keep the crazymakers from breaking into the sensitive places where you store your most precious moments. Let's take a long look at why it is important to understand how to use boundaries.

Meet Ella the Umbrella

Ella MacDonald was a gentle soul who worked hard at everything she did. Employers loved her because Ella never complained. She kept plowing no matter how hard the field became. If a letter came in late in the day, Ella stayed and typed it until the work was done if it meant she was the last to leave the office. Like a big umbrella that covers everything coming across the desk, Ella did it . . . when it was way beyond what was justifiable and right!

One evening Ella came home late from the office. Her roommate was sitting at the dining-room table in their apartment.

"You look beat," the roommate said.

Ella plopped down in the nearest chair. "I'm so tired, I feel like I could fall asleep in five seconds."

The roommate frowned. "This is the third night this week that you've come home so late. What's going on down there in that office?"

"Nothing in particular. A few of my supervisors seem to drop this work in my lap at the last minute, and I guess I can't say no."

"Why?" the roommate asked. "This is crazy. Obviously these people don't exercise any respect for you."

"Oh, no!" Ella said defensively. "I don't think they are inconsiderate."

"Listen. You tell me why they couldn't have gotten these requests to you much earlier in the day—or why you couldn't let them wait until morning."

Ella looked sheepish. "I don't know," she answered. "I don't seem to know how to protect myself."

"I think you're putting it mildly. You don't know how to *defend* yourself!"

Ella the umbrella felt powerless, and it showed in her worn-out condition.

Recovering Power

Crazymakers are able to be destructive by targeting people who don't have a good sense of their own strength or capacities. The truth is that many of us have never considered how important it is to maintain a sense of our own ability. Without power we are at the mercy of anyone . . . as was Ella.

Crazymakers often function with coercive patterns that induce pain and make us comply because of an implied threat of retribution. While we certainly are not interested in encouraging you to respond by creating fear of the difficult person, you do need to maintain an awareness of your own capacities. Recovering power is an important dimension of sidestepping the onslaught of people with a diminished capacity to care. Boundaries will help accomplish this goal.

Meet Ken Merrill, a guy who will help you understand how important boundaries can be. Ken first showed up in a Meier Clinic day program after he had survived a two-day coma from a drug overdose. Obviously, Ken was in bad shape and needed help.

Ken's plunge downward began following his dismissal from the Army for having a narcissistic personality disorder. The military discovered Ken had a significant capacity for causing trouble when he was upset. During a conversation with a superior officer, Ken lipped off in arrogant terms, demanding to be promoted to a higher rank. After becoming more than irritated, the officer turned him over to other officers who attempted to calm him down and get him under control. Unfortunately, Ken became more animated and the conversations only exploded.

In the end, his behavior became so disruptive that Ken received a dishonorable discharge.

Ken Merrill was particularly devastated because for years he had wanted to be in the Army. His father was a decorated veteran of the Korean War, and his medals added emphasis to Ken's desire to wear a uniform. Interestingly enough, Ken had a relatively normal childhood and had not been in trouble at home when he was growing up.

After Ken was discharged, he continued his abusive rampage, offending almost everyone he encountered. His bombastic tirades knocked other people around as if they were bowling pins. He finally sank into a horrendous depression that resulted in an attempted suicide.

When Dr. Paul Meier attended Ken, he thoroughly examined his new patient's background. On the medical charts, Dr. Meier noticed that Ken had been adopted as a child. Aspects of Ken's behavior simply didn't match up with his normal development as a child. Something was missing, and maybe it was hidden in the mother who had given birth to him.

Dr. Meier started researching where Ken had come from and began to find unexpected evidence emerge about Ken's birth mother: she had a bipolar disorder. Suddenly the pieces came together. Ken's narcissistic behavior was related to a mental problem he had unknowingly inherited. His unfortunate conduct had not come from his emotional development as a child, but through the bloodstream. Ken was struggling with tendencies that he didn't know how to control.

Is this frequent? Unfortunately, 70 percent of bipolar personalities never get diagnosed or treated. Often, they slide into alcoholism or become drug addicts. Like Ken, they are very nice people most of the time, but have "manic" times when they can get in trouble without understanding what is surging through their minds. But how *are you* going to deal with such an individual, particularly when you have no idea of what is going on? (For more information on bipolar and other genetic disorders that influence behavior, read *Mood Swings* by Dr. Paul Meier, Dr. Frank Minirth, and Stephen Arterburn.)

In Ken's case, he was treated with antidepressant and mood-stabilizing drugs that helped him return to a normal life. On these medications he was always quite nice and reasonable. Ken's friends and parents became his "support group" who insisted that he stay on these drugs for the rest of his life, since getting off them would almost certainly result in a recurrence of Ken's inherited chemical imbalance in his brain and bring back his "false narcissism."

In order to find your personal power and set boundaries, you need to identify the emotions that made you feel so powerless. The following are six of the most common negative emotions people experience when they are intimidated. Ken Merrill certainly caused his friends to feel some of these emotions during his "manic" cycle.

The Big Six Emotions

Look at the list below carefully and see if any reflect your condition. When an area fits, leave a check mark. Check as many areas as you feel are appropriate.

○ *1. Fear.* Fear may come with a name or it may be a nameless anxiety that you feel when you sense a problem can turn into pain. You may worry subtly or your concerns can turn into fright and intense apprehension. Regardless of how it originates, you know that a crazymaker facilitates fear in your heart.

Think back to your psychological assessment in Chapter 10. Is there an incident there or a person there who elicited the same kind of fear? If so, how did you respond then?

_____

_____

_____

Is that an adequate response now? If not, how would you change it?

_____

_____

_____

If you want a more complete understanding of your fears and anxieties, you might wish to read *Fear Less for Life* by Stephen Arterburn, Dr. Paul Meier, and Dr. Robert Wise.

○ *2. Anger.* Often the difficult people in your world cross the boundaries or lines of propriety that you expect others to observe. When the rules, principles, standards, or guidelines you live by are violated, you become angry. You may not necessarily express how upset you are publicly. In fact, you may even repress your anger, which causes it to come back as depression.

Again think back to your assessment in Chapter 10. Did you uncover anger in your past? What caused it? Write your answer in the space below.

_____

_____

_____

How did you respond then?

_____

_____

_____

Is that an adequate response you could use now? If not, how would you change it?

_____

_____

_____

○ *3. Inadequacy.* Often we carry feelings of awkwardness or inability from our childhoods; this inadequacy is tapped when a crazymaker starts drilling holes in our skulls. Rather than getting angry, we feel our inabilities have been exposed.

We cower because of our feelings of inadequacy. Abusive behavior can cause us to feel we've been sent to the closet for an enforced time-out!

While doing your assessment in Chapter 10 did you discover moments when you felt inadequate? If so, how did you respond then?

_____

_____

_____

Is this feeling of inadequacy contributing to your feelings now? If so, how might you change this?

_____

_____

_____

○ *4. Guilt.* No one knows what percentage of the population grew up feeling guilty, but the figures could be staggering. Many of us had parents who instilled a sense of culpability in us; everything that went wrong was in some way or the other our fault! Today we naturally assume every wrong turn in the road has to have been our fault. A skillful crazymaker can hit that note in us every time.

In your assessment in Chapter 10 did you discover people who made you feel guilty? Who are they?

_____

_____

_____

How did you respond then?

_____

_____

_____

Are your present feelings of guilt because of selfish acts you have done that hurt others, or are your present feelings of guilt influenced by these past occurrences? If so, how?

_____

_____

_____

Many suffer from false guilt, which means feeling guilty for things that were actually *not* your fault, such as being molested, date raped, abused, or even simply existing when you received various "don't exist" messages from a parent, mate, or others. Try to think of examples.

_____

_____

_____

How can you change that so you will not be hooked by a crazymaker in the future?

_____

_____

_____

○ *5. Frustration.* Frustration grows out of a sense of not being able to accomplish what we believed we should have (or what our crazymaker is pressuring us to accomplish). It's not that we feel the problem is our inability; rather, we simply haven't run hard enough to clear the last hurdle. We feel irritated, unsettled, and nullified. At the end of the day, we leave the office feeling as if we simply haven't done enough or been enough.

Again think back to your assessment. Did you uncover some moments when you felt frustrated? Describe these moments in the space below.

_____

_____

_____

How did you respond at that time?

_____

_____

_____

Could your response in the past be influencing how you respond to the crazymaker in your life today? If so, how can you change this response in the future?

_____

_____

_____

○ *6. Hurt.* Unseen, throbbing pain deep down in the pit of our stomachs erupts when someone is emotionally tearing our heads off. We have a sense of loss. Maybe we can't identify what it is, but we feel stepped on and unappreciated. Probably as many people in a business office have this experience as any other feeling.

Again think back to your assessment. Did you uncover people who hurt you or moments when you were hurt? If so, list the people and/or the moments in the space below:

_____

_____

_____

Could people or situations from your past be influencing the way you are responding to the crazymaker in your life today? If so, how can you change this response in the future?

_____

_____

_____

These emotions are the Big Six. The list certainly isn't exhaustive, and you may have discovered a different emotion than what we identified. Which of your feelings do crazymakers hit when they run into you? Think it through carefully because identifying your pain clarifies where the first of your boundaries will be built. Now let's consider how we can erect those walls of protection.

Putting Up the Fence

Step 1: What do I need to protect? If someone crowds in front of you in a lane of traffic, you may not like it, but in five seconds the irritation is gone. When a difficult person screams at you in an elevator full of people, you'll still be fuming the next day. Makes a difference, doesn't it? Some aspects of our emotional lives are negotiable; others aren't. The question is, "*Where* is your pain zone?" Think back to the six areas you just finished examining and identify what you found to be your area of vulnerability in a current situation with your crazymaker.

Do you feel . . .

○ fearful?

○ angry?

○ inadequate?

○ guilty?

○ frustrated?

○ hurt?

This is your pain zone, the area or areas in which you are vulnerable, where you need protection.

For example, as Jack Smith thought about what happened to him when Ann went into one of her attacks, he discovered his own feelings of deep inadequacy.

Step 2: What was damaged in the attack? When the crazymaker swoops down on your desk, you generally aren't prepared for the bombs to go off under your feet. Only later can you reflect on what's happened and make some sense out of the assault. As you think about why you were so upset, the second area to clarify is *what* was damaged in the attack.

Jack Smith pushed further into his memories and realized that continual conflicts with Ann had damaged his self-esteem. Over a period of time, his diminished sense of self-worth spilled over into every other relationship in his life. *Damage control meant that he had to build a fence around his self-esteem.*

You may find that it takes more time than you would have thought to fully understand what is diminished when an insensitive person cuts into you. Writing about it in a journal or thinking about this as you are driving down the road may prove helpful and important.

Look at your own area of vulnerability by filling in the blanks in the sentence below:

I feel _____ when a crazymaker attacks me because this person is damaging my _____.

Step 3: What is my bottom line? As you clarify your damaged emotions when the attack occurred, you may also become aware that the crazymaker has operated as if he or she has all the power. If the difficult person owns the company you work for, you know who calls the final shot. What happens when you discover someone who has "no give"?

The Ken Merrills of this world can pose bone-breaking problems. Regardless of what causes their behavior, you must have a clear sense of what you will and will not tolerate. Actually, the Army gave Ken a clear bottom line. They would not allow him to be a crazymaker. His parents had to set similar boundaries. Ken would take his pills, or he would have to move out of their home. If he began acting with the grandiosity exhibited in the military, they would confront him about his extreme behavior. Ken agreed that he would recognize their intentions were only for his best interest, and he would listen.

Often narcissists focus on image and care little about

feelings, so they may not give any slack. What then? That's the point at which it's essential for you to know your bottom line. You must clarify your own personal "when"!

Women in business and politics are treated better today because a few women drew a line and said, "No more." Sexual harassment has serious consequences now because people came to realize this violation of human dignity is a serious boundary not to be crossed.

Jack Smith determined his bottom line. He would not allow Ann to undercut his worth as a human being. Jack found a three-by-five-inch card and wrote out, "Regardless of who attacks me, I remain a human being of inestimable worth. Because Jesus died for me, no one can reduce my importance to God. No one will rob me of self-esteem."

Jack came to the conclusion that his spouse had to be stopped from undermining his self-esteem. Jack realized this was the point where he needed to draw a line in the sand.

Ann usually began torpedoing Jack by narrowing her eyes in a menacing stare. She had the ability to glare at him as if he were an insignificant child. In the past, her posture sent him into a panic. Next, Ann would follow with a statement like, "You idiot!" or "You're such a moron!" Instantly, Jack would feel like a fool. The hardened look and her insult had become Ann's one-two punch, which floored him every time. Jack had to set a boundary to stop these assaults on his personal self-worth.

Jack Smith decided that the first moment Ann narrowed her eyes, he would immediately give himself a silent mental message: *Stand firm and don't believe what you hear.* By simply saying this statement to himself, Jack could thwart the negative feelings that always boiled up and overwhelmed him. The sentence also took his attention away from the threat Ann was attempting to impose on him.

A new boundary immediately followed Ann's barbs. He decided that he would immediately interrupt her and say, "I am not an idiot or a moron. You are using these demeaning phrases to divert my attention from the real problem." If Ann called him a name again, Jack decided he would repeat the sentence and refuse to discuss the matter until Ann changed her posture.

Did the boundary work? Ann was so befuddled that at first she had a difficult time responding. Eventually she changed her approach, never realizing that Jack had not only reclaimed his self-worth, but also set a perimeter that stopped her from undercutting it.

You need to find your similar bottom line. The more clearly you understand that position, the more power you will have. Remember our friend Ella the umbrella? After much thought and consideration, Ella MacDonald decided she would accept no new work after 3:45 every afternoon. She had a right to leave at 5:00 like everyone else. The company could take it or leave it!

Much to her surprise, Ella discovered that within two weeks, her superiors in the office changed how they related to her. She also received more respect among her peers. Her fellow employees had decided that Ella mattered . . . because Ella made it clear *that she did!* Ella had come to a hard but firm decision. If she was pushed on this issue, Ella was prepared to terminate her job. She had found her bottom line.

While you may have never clarified your stopping point or discussed your boundaries with another person, you have some line that you either will not cross or know you should never violate. Constant assault from a crazymaker mandates that you clarify where the "don't violate" zone is, and then make the decision that you will enforce the consequences *when* violations occurs.

At some point, you will need to put your foot down. Clarifying the alternatives is determining the place where your foot is going to land. This doesn't mean that you have to become a pugnacious person. In fact, putting your foot down can mean simply walking away.

Let's put it another way. Do you think God wants you to be unprotected? Is it His will to leave you without an oar in a boat heading for the waterfalls? Nothing in Scripture supports that point of view. Our heavenly Father's love intends for you to live a fulfilling, happy life. Don't ever doubt His plan.

What are your alternatives? What is your bottom line? In the space provided below, write out some of the new lines you are drawing in the sand.

_____

_____

_____

Step 4: Put the protective boundaries in cement. Crazy-making is not a hobby for the person attacking you; therefore change can't be a part-time or temporary project for you. You must make a decision that you are going to live a new lifestyle. Rather than letting yourself fall back into old, destructive patterns, you must make the decision to stay permanently on your new path.

Please don't misunderstand us. We're not suggesting you decide to become a relentless, hard-nosed prizefighter. In fact, it's our hope that everything you are doing is motivated by love. You can still care about what happens with a narcissist and hope for the best for him or her. However, that doesn't mean you continue allowing the crazymaker to run over you with a truck. Now is the time. This is the moment to set your boundaries in concrete terms.

Make a definite, unbending decision about where you will stand regardless of what happens. Please pray about the decision, and then declare your new stance by completing the statement on the lines below.

I will never_____

_____

_____

_____.

Latching the Gate

Like an old gate into a cow field, you have to shut the latch if you want to keep the cows in! You are changing pastures. No longer will you be a victim. You've decided to be an authentic person. Can you do it? Sure. But you've got to keep the gate shut. Now's the time to protect what is yours. You've got the power. Do it!

Our second step out of the chaos is to learn to set effective boundaries.

chapter TWELVE

Step Three: Encourage Counseling

In *Stop Walking on Eggshells*, Paul Mason and Randi Kreger's excellent book on borderline personality disorder, they observe that people generally respond to difficult persons in one of two ways: *They either become sponges or mirrors!* This choice makes all the difference in how crazymakers react to them.

"Sponge-types" absorb and soak up the rage and hostility poured out on them, feeling it is best to absorb the abuse; these people don't realize that "sponges" only perpetuate the attack. On the other hand, "mirror-types" do not hesitate to reflect back the negative emotions and all the hurtful feelings aimed at them. They attempt to help crazymakers feel what is lurking below the surface of their anger. Without getting snared into impossible accusations, blaming, criticism, and demands, "mirror-types" maintain a steady direction, reflecting back what was aimed at them.

Mason and Kreger's point is that you must have a definite sense of direction to keep the boat on the right course or you will get nowhere. "Mirroring" is part of that voyage. We couldn't agree more. Crazymakers must be navigated toward help. If anyone needs counseling, it's these folks. We believe you would be helped by learning to be an effective mirror of the chaos in order to help crazymakers see their need.

Sally Harris and Jack Smith needed to continually mirror their home-life problems to their spouses. Mirroring is simply obeying the biblical urge to "speak the truth in love" (Ephesians 4:15). In psychiatric terms, it is called "processing." For example, in group therapy sessions at Dr. Meier's Day Program, when one patient shares about a painful event in her life, the other group members are encouraged to think and feel out loud, sharing not only their empathy toward the person, but also any personal factual or emotional memories that come to mind. It also implies sometimes saying back to the sharer what you think you heard that person saying to be sure you understood correctly. These things are included in "processing" or "mirroring."

Sally struggled with George's resistance to counseling. He would go for one or two times and then not return. Jack

Smith was unable to get Ann to enter the counseling process with him at all. Her claim was, "You've got the problem, not me."

The Struggle with Limited Insight

Mirroring requires Sally and Jack telling George and Ann the truth, in a loving way, about what they see their mates doing or not doing and how Sally and Jack feel about it. Both Jack Smith and Sally Harris were actually battling with another characteristic of a crazymaker. *Crazymakers have limited insight!*

In their minds' eyes, the problems swirling around crazymakers don't have anything to do with them. Often they will genuinely seem to be mystified by other peoples' insistence that something has gone wrong with them. *They don't have the problem; you do!* Second verse, same as the first.

Crazymakers lack insight because they constantly worry about tarnishing their images. Their preoccupation with getting their best foot forward keeps vision of their problems at such a low level that they cannot see what is obvious to everyone else.

Encouragement is extremely important, because they need reassurance that their seriously examining these areas of tension will not diminish who they are. Working out hidden emotional needs actually leads toward greater maturity and an increased sense of our identity. But it can be a challenge to empower a crazymaker to see this. We believe it would be helpful for you to become an effective mirror of the chaos in order to help the crazymakers see their need for counseling. Everyone grows through the counseling experience.

How to Recommend Counseling

Earlier we offered an important insight. *Crazymakers do not usually do well when they are confronted.* Hitting difficult people head-on is more likely to produce a bump on your forehead than facilitating insight in them. Confronting these people demands more of an "end run" approach, remembering that they deeply fear being embarrassed or being made to look inadequate. You must approach them from their blind side if you want to make a significant impression. Solomon told us (Proverbs 9:8) that if we rebuke a fool, he will only hate us for doing so, so don't waste your time with him.

For a moment consider how a professional therapist operates. You may not have been part of one of these sessions, so let us describe the setting that could be expected if you came into one of the Meier Clinics. Pay close attention to the components of *how* care is offered.

First, you would be greeted by a warm, cheerful person who treats you like a special person. No one leaves a hint that something is wrong with you. Regardless of what brought you to the clinic, you would be received not as someone with a problem, but as a friend.

Second, during the intake process you would be given an examination, similar to the self-examination in Chapter 10. Nothing about this process would put you in an awkward position except sharing incidents of past abuse (or past failures) to a caring professional. Again, you would seem to be in the driver's seat, answering questions because you are comfortable, not sharing anything you choose not to share yet.

Third, when the results of the psychological tests are interpreted, the therapist would ask you questions, saying, "Does this sound like you?" Rather than confronting you with harsh results, the doctor, nurse, or therapist would gently ask your thoughts about *what the test seems to indicate*. No counselor would demand that you accept his or her personal definition of the truth. As the discussion continued, a defiant or frightened client would slowly, but clearly, begin to see the need in his or her life.

Nothing places the crazymaker on the hot seat. The therapist's kind, thoughtful responses puts the person at ease, preparing him or her to come to his or her own conclusions and insights. This is the approach we have to use if we are going to help difficult people define a new direction for their lives.

Fourth, another indirect approach counselors use is to ask the person to read a book, articles, or a well-written description of a problem like his or her own issue, and then return to the clinic with a response. For example, Hal Straus and Dr. Jerold Kreisman's little book *I Hate You, Don't Leave Me; Understanding Borderline Personality Disorder* probes issues of violent mood swings, chronic depression, and the tendency to attack people. The problems are examined in a sensitive manner that exposes the undercurrents running through a troubled person's life.

When the crazymaker returns, the therapist would act casually. "Did you find any parts of the book affecting you?" the counselor might ask. Often the clients will find tears in their eyes, and some may have difficulty expressing the pain they are feeling because the literature had touched their nerves.

When reading such a work, difficult people begin to recognize the emptiness and need in their own lives. Again, the message is sneaking up on them from their blind sides. They often wake up to the importance of loving and being loved, see what they have missed out on by being narcissistic, and genuinely repent.

These examples will probably spark other insights on your part. You will be able to come up with your own approaches that fit the difficult persons you must confront;

and we will suggest some in the next section. In the meantime, remember these beginning guidelines:

1. Don't embarrass the crazymaker.

2. Image is everything to a crazymaker, so don't diminish the facade he or she wears.

3. Find an indirect approach; it pays dividends.

4. Remember the goal is to help the person accept the need for professional help.

Counseling for Difficult People

Let's be clear about the problem we are trying to correct. The amount of counseling needed to bring insight to a crazymaker depends on the seriousness of his or her problem. Difficult people may simply lack insight into how their comments hurt people. However, their lack of feeling for other people must be addressed, either by a friend or by a counselor.

Jane Parker constantly made snide comments at the end of any discussion with her friends. She would wait until an issue seemed completely settled, and then fire a barb at someone who had disagreed with her. During this particular gathering, Jane verbally assaulted Renee, who was new to their group. Afterward, Jane's friend, Sandi, approached her.

"Jane," Sandi said, kindly but matter-of-factly, "I need to ask you about something that worries me."

"Sure." Jane sounded as indifferent as usual.

"Do you even like, or care about, Renee as a person?"

Jane blinked several times. "I . . . I . . . don't know what you mean." She sounded genuinely bewildered.

"I'm not trying to be critical, and I don't want to hurt your feelings, but I'm not sure you realize that your final comments in this discussion today cut Renee to the quick."

For a second a knowing look flashed across Jane's eyes, indicating she understood what Sandi was talking about. The look faded, but Jane didn't say anything.

"I'd like to make a suggestion, Jane. I have a friend who helps people develop sensitivity. She helps them learn to hear more effectively. I think you'd receive some valuable assistance. Could we talk about your spending some time with my friend?"

Jane stared. After a long pause she said thoughtfully. "You think I need help?"

"I'm not trying to crawl under your skin, but a therapist helped me become aware of some important aspects of my behavior, and I profited from the time with her. I believe you'd do the same. I believe it would help *you* to enjoy life more."

Sandi had been sensitive but direct. Without embarrassing Jane, she made it clear that help was needed. Jane didn't say much, but she knew what Sandi was talking about. A door was opened.

Some difficult people will require continued counseling to change how they confront others. The issue is getting them to recognize that they tend to be indifferent to other people's pain. Opening their eyes to indifference is not easy. Like seeing the back of your head, the problems aren't observable without someone mirroring back the truth to the one who is blind to his or her own behavior.

Counseling for the Narcissist

Narcissists will often take a great deal of time before they become open and improve. You should anticipate a difficult struggle to get these people into counseling. Further, narcissists require long-term care, sometimes several years, to start turning around their lack of concern. They have unfortunately learned how to manipulate people rather than dealing honestly with others' feelings. Because narcissists can be treacherous, they may battle with a therapist for a considerable amount of time before they start to open up even slightly. The Day Program helps them much more quickly, because they are "bombarded" with the truth, seven hours a day, five days a week for three weeks or more, by an entire team of therapists and other patients. They either quit their denial or get away and leave in a huff.

Often narcissists start to change after a crisis has forced them into a corner and given them no other alternatives. Faced with a catastrophe, their pain surfaces, and they seek the help that can only come from the honest acceptance of the therapist.

Trish Mason's friends had thinned out the older she became. Trish was always open to taking something from them, but never gave anyone anything in return. She had a cold, hard streak and a tendency to hurt people. Trish listened to no one. She was good at manipulating people, but the art of friendship had never been learned. However, Trish came to a turning point when her only son, Stan, was killed in a car wreck.

Stan was a traveling sales rep. One day his car hit a patch of ice on the highway, skidding into a tree. Since Trish was already widowed, she now found herself alone in the world. Grief and brokenness settled over her like a black cloud. Two months after Stan's funeral, Rev. Jim Jarrell from the church came to see her. He caught Trish at a moment when she had been crying.

"I know this time has been particularly difficult for you," Reverend Jarrell said.

Trish nodded. "At my age, the loss of a child is unbearable. Stan was all I had left in the world." She cried for a moment. "No one ever calls me." Trish stopped and dried her eyes. "Reverend, why don't any of my friends even call me on the phone?"

The minister paused for a moment and studied the white-haired woman. He knew Trish Mason well and sensed this was the time to be direct and forthright. "Do you want an honest answer?" he asked.

"Of course!" Trish snapped.

"You won't like it," Jarrell said. "And you will probably be offended with me, but I'll tell you the truth if you really want to hear it."

Trish stared at her minister for a moment. Her eyes had returned to their usual hardness, but she also looked more vulnerable than usual. "I know something is wrong," she said resolutely, "and I can't figure out what it is. Yes, I'll listen to what you tell me."

Reverend Jarrell nodded his head. "I'm not trying to put you on the spot or make you uncomfortable. You understand?"

"Yes. Go on."

"I have a friend who could help you understand why many of your relationships have failed. You would be helped by talking with him."

Trish stiffened. "That isn't what I expected to hear."

"But you told me to be honest."

Trish's shoulders dropped. "Yes," she said. "I did. Go on with what you were saying."

The minister continued and encouraged Trish Mason to seek help. If it had not been for the current crisis, she would not have listened, but her pain opened her eyes to see that she needed help. And she found it at a Christian counseling center.

The point is basic. Whether you are dealing with a difficult person or a full-blown narcissist, your crazymaker needs consistent encouragement in two crucial areas: to get into counseling and to stay there. He or she must be fortified to maintain the sessions in a counselor's office. Loving support from a spouse or friend makes a vital difference.

Creating Change

People often ask us, "What form of therapy will keep a crazymaker in a counseling process?" Obviously, relating in a personal and intimate way with a specific counselor is vital, but many times it is difficult to get troubled people across the office threshold. We have found that the method called "group process" makes an easier starting point and is frequently more effective than individual therapy.

Directed by trained therapists, these group sessions

usually run for ninety minutes. During the meetings, participants discuss their issues on as frank a level as is comfortable for them. They begin wherever they are, and no one pushes them into a bind. As time goes by, the clients begin to trust each other and talk more openly. They dare to venture out, talking about their deeper issues. Slowly the trust and caring of the group allows all the members to finally address the basic concerns in their lives. The clients, guided by skilled group therapists, learn to think and feel out loud with each other.

The role of the therapist is to keep the group on track and offer appropriate and valid insights at the right time, while also protecting clients from an occasional rude narcissist in the group. But in most of our therapy groups, the clients are usually wonderful, intelligent, and caring people, some of whom have been victims of abusive past relationships. Group members often make helpful and important suggestions. Narcissists slowly but surely begin to hear the counsel needed to help them and recognize what has gone wrong in their lives. Often process groups discuss spiritual issues, adding this element to the climate for change.

Because process groups are so accepting, self-absorbed people are encouraged to stay with the program. The support of a larger circle of friends who continue to care provides the sustaining reassurance these crazymakers need.

Comforting the Bold and the Bad

You may like what you've been reading but still feel terrified that you will not be able to pull off the task. The truth is you may not. Let's frankly look at this possibility and be totally honest.

No matter how creative and positive the environment may be, how helpful the staff, how clever the professional response to the client, at least 10 percent of the clients in the Meier Clinics' Day Program drop out quickly. We are not dealing with an easy problem when confronting difficult people. Many run away from the truth as fast as they can, using all sorts of excuses to "save face" back home.

You know how formidable these adversaries can be! And their attacks on you have become serious enough that you must be willing to risk failure. In fact, *risk* is the price that must be paid if change is to follow. There simply is no other route to take.

One of the advantages of a professional Christian counseling center is that it clearly offers a Christian context for all that is said and done. This setting automatically allows a counselor clear permission to deal with spiritual issues, and this often opens doors unexpectedly. Some secular therapists actually *encourage* narcissism to the "Me Generation." They carry "assertiveness training," which can be good, to a bad extreme and reward selfishness.

For example, Ann Smith and George Harris were unquestionably people who had made a Christian commitment. The Meier Clinic staff knew Ann and George had Christian values that could be accessed if it would help therapy. This also opened up new possibilities to encourage Ann and George to stay with the program.

In the New Testament, the book of James offers strong admonition to reinforce a decision to become involved in counseling. The book says:

Is anyone among you suffering? Let him pray. . . . Is anyone among you sick? Let him call for the elders of the church . . . Confess your trespasses to one another, and pray for one another, that you may be healed." (James 5:13–16)

Confessing personal sins and the sins of narcissists against you is an amazingly powerful healing agent.

Often narcissistic spouses with spiritual values can begin to see counseling in a new light when they think of the sharing process as being much like "confessing our sin" or our deepest need to another faithful person. Truthfully, therapy *is* confessing our most frightening and overwhelming hidden defects to a confidential friend. Saying the words out loud can be where the process of change begins. Jerks also become aware of being jerks and confess their jerky behaviors to the group. Then they are loved with open arms and applauded for being vulnerable human beings.

They may be bold and bad, but these people still need our encouragement to get into therapy! Let's encourage them.

Our third step out of chaos is to encourage getting in and staying with counseling.

chapter THIRTEEN

Step Four:
Find Friends to Support
You in the Battle

After some counseling by himself, Jack Smith gained enough insight and self-esteem that he was ready to confront Ann's behavior. He had come to see how much of her bluster was an attempt to stay in control and exercise power. Jack started pushing Ann to join him in therapy.

Sure enough! The missiles started falling!

Ann's usual anger went up a notch on the scale, and a new cycle of behavior began to emerge. Beforehand, when Jack had strongly insisted that their marriage needed outside help, Ann had always been resistant and difficult. However on this go-around, Jack decided he wouldn't back off.

Planting his feet firmly, he maintained that the issue wasn't negotiable.

How did Jack become so decisive? A new dimension had entered his life over the three months preceding this battle. He had become part of a support group that also held him accountable. While Ann didn't realize what this small group meant to Jack, he had found a new way to muster the strength he needed. A group of men were standing with him.

Eventually a nasty explosion occurred, which ended in a traumatic fight. After the smoke cleared the next day, it was obvious Ann had dramatically overplayed her hand. Jack was still visibly determined. Ann could see she needed to regroup.

"I'm sorry," Ann said with genuine contrition in her voice. "The fight last night was entirely my fault."

Jack listened, not saying anything. He started thinking through what he had learned in therapy, assessing how best to respond.

"Please forgive me!" Ann burst out emotionally. "I'm a fool, Jack. A terrible pig-headed fool!" She threw herself in his arms and hugged him tightly.

Jack put his arms around her, but kept thinking about the best reply. He didn't want her to cry and certainly wished the fight would go away, but he had learned to listen carefully.

"I can't live without you," Ann begged. "Let's simply put all of this quarreling behind us *and start over!*"

Those last words jarred Jack. *Start over* was a phrase that Ann used when she actually meant, *"forget what I said and did, and don't bring it up again."* Putting the disagreement behind them was only a ploy to avoid talking about the actual problems that still existed.

A few days passed and then another cycle of behavior would start again. However, now he would not allow Ann to get off the hook. His message was always the same. *You will go with me to counseling or else.*

Jack was standing on new ground previously unknown to Ann. His message to her was "go or good-bye." Of course, self-absorbed people explode like skyrockets under these circumstances, but Jack meant what he was saying. When a crisis is reached, and a line is drawn in the sand, often crazymakers will knuckle under because the cost is higher than they are willing to pay.

While Ann had little choice but to capitulate, she didn't relent about how therapy felt to her after her counseling began. When she expressed her feelings, they were consistently the same. "I don't need to be here; Jack does." Becoming increasingly angry, she released her hostility in overt ways. She was upset to reveal their problems to a counselor! She maintained a steady, boiling hostility because she didn't believe she needed what the therapist was dishing out. Finally, Ann remained angry with Jack for making her participate in the process. Her dissatisfaction didn't stop, but

Ann was forced to enter counseling—thanks to Jack's supportive friends behind the scenes.

Finding Support

In the time that Jack Smith was in counseling, a number of new relationships developed in his life—and they made a tremendous difference. First, Jack's counselor had become a consistent friend who offered the warmth of Christian care. No matter what happened, the counselor would stand with him and walk through the problems with firm consistency. Jack had a professional shoulder to lean on.

Second, Jack had a number of pastor friends in his area who were trustworthy and reliable. One particular pastor at a neighboring church offered all the time that was needed to sit in a coffee shop and simply listen. Jack could speak freely and share his heart, knowing all matters would be held in confidence. On many of these occasions, the pastor prayed with Jack and assured him that his prayers wouldn't stop.

Jack had acquired the personal support he needed to keep on marching when the bombs were falling at home. While advice and insight were important, the encouragement he received from sustaining friends gave him the emotional endurance to continue facing his marriage problems.

Why Support Helps

Loners do not do well in their battles with difficult people and narcissists. And fear grows fast in solitude. Having someone else in the trenches can make a significant difference in our endurance. There are far-reaching benefits in joining a support group.

Everyone needs emotional support. When you are standing alone, there is no one to offer encouragement or pats on the back. However, others give us the inspiration we need to go on. A support group can add an enormous element of strength.

Emotional support gives us a place to cry. Because difficult people often injure us, we may need the loving support of friends who can put an arm around our shoulders when we have come to the breaking point. When Sally Harris realized her husband, George, would never reliably attend counseling sessions, she knew she needed a support system outside her home.

Emotional support gives us a place to test our perceptions. The confusion that crazymakers generate will many times leave us disoriented and unsure of ourselves. It's difficult to climb out of that hole entirely by ourselves. We need other hands to pull us out of the ditch by telling us how they more objectively see our problem. They can give us greater confidence in our own opinions.

In Patricia Evans's book, *The Verbally Abusive Relationship*, she describes one of the values that the emotional support of a group can offer. She notes that identifying and naming the "problem" is an important part of what a therapist can do for us. That same function can also be a gift from an emotional support group. We need to know what is wrong with our relationships in the clearest and most simple terms, and other people's insights can help us find a strong base on which to stand. Often, the simple task of having friends ask questions about our struggle will help us find insights that previously eluded us.

Millions of alcoholics testify to the power of Alcoholic Anonymous (AA) groups to sustain them through difficult times when they fear their addiction will defeat them. Two of the key reasons these AA groups are so powerful is that alcoholics make a decision that they are powerless over their problems and then decide to turn their wills and their lives over to the power of God. We may feel humiliated to admit that we cannot deal with a crazymaker, but that decision could be the start of a new capacity for spiritual strength if it results in inviting God to have an increased part in our thoughts, decisions, and actions. By asking God for more wisdom and insight, we gain more awareness of the truth.

In a similar fashion, another one of the important groups that have helped multitudes of people is the Al-Anon program. While these groups are primarily to sustain people who have family members with drinking problems, Al-Anon teaches members how to become independent of emotional entanglements that are often similar to narcissistic problems. This program frequently helps people who have codependent relationships unravel the mystery of how their lives have developed unseen entanglements that drag them down.

Thousands of churches also have home-sharing groups where people gather to discuss their issues, pray together, and then come back the following week to share their progress in facing these problems. Millions of strugglers can testify that home meetings have made the difference in their overcoming issues that previously defeated them.

Men and women often find similar sustaining support through groups that gather for discussion or Bible study. These groups may deal with topics unrelated to emotional issues, but they still offer insight and affection that help lift a person like Jack Smith during hard times. At the least, these groups can help neutralize the discomfort experienced by someone in a crazymaker relationship.

Could these groups help you? Absolutely. It is essential that a group maintain a code of confidentiality, safeguarding each member's need for spiritual covering. Once you know that the members of a group can be trusted, you will be able to lean on these good people and allow them to help you walk through your dark time.

Turning the Heat Off

Jack Smith found that his group of faithful friends gave him the extra strength he needed. These men kept their eye on Jack and sustained him when he had to live through crazy-making at home. Their supportive words helped him realize he could confront Ann's criticisms. Rather than simply walking out of the room, Jack came to see that he must stop allowing himself to be Ann's target. He had to plant his feet in front of her and turn back the barrage. This discernment proved to be important, and a number of decisions followed.

First, Jack Smith decided that he must stand up to Ann's criticism during therapy. When she continued to proclaim that there was no need for her to be in counseling, Ann was not facing reality. The therapist completely supported Jack in this matter. No matter how resistant she became, Ann *did* need to talk about her problems. Her attacks were attempts to avoid the truth or ploys to avoid responsibility. No matter how heated their exchanges became, Jack stopped backing down.

Second, Jack would not allow any camouflaging of the facts. Ann's assaults on him were highly inappropriate. In order to maintain this position, Jack recognized the necessity of changing how he responded to his wife. The counselor helped Jack formulate a new way of communicating. When Ann started expressing anger, Jack developed an immediate response. He would listen for a moment and then say, "I'm sure you believe what you said is true, but here are the facts." He would then proceed to talk in objective factual terms, laying out evidence to support his position.

At the outset Ann didn't seem to hear anything he said, but that didn't stop Jack's approach. He would respond again, "I'm sure you believe your position is true, but . . ." and then he would state the facts once more. His consistent retort didn't change, regardless of what Ann said. Jack no longer felt on the defensive. He was beginning to get back on a level playing field.

As he denied Ann's warped description of past events, Jack began to regain his emotional balance and soon found a new sense of security. In turn, Ann began to see that throwing dust in the air did nothing but get dirt on her face. In the midst of these battles, Jack could reclaim his identity as a truthful person.

Jack also began to identify other components in Ann's attacks. Her anger was often accusatory, blaming him for everything. In many instances, these emotional explosions seemed to come out of nowhere, and Jack felt no undercurrent of warmth or concern. He could think back over many of their confrontations and still not see any reason for why they happened. Sticking to the truth had helped Jack realize how unfounded much of Ann's anger actually was.

Both Jack Smith and Sally Harris discovered how important it was to develop a community of caring, good friends who would surround them with love and affection. Jack and Sally no longer only sought support from their immediate families, but developed a broader, wider range of intelligent, loving Christian friends. Even if they had to go to services alone, a church with confidential support helped each of them remember that they were not standing by themselves in this struggle. While many of their new friends had no idea what was happening at home, they remained a sustaining force in Sally's and Jack's lives.

Clients who have become involved in small church groups tell us that the loving ministry of people who not only listen, but also pray for them imparts invaluable encouragement. They find the spiritual endurance that equips them to keep on walking even when a crazymaker has tried to cut their legs off. You need these friends on your path!

Our fourth step out of chaos is to find the emotional and spiritual encouragement we need from other people.

chapter FOURTEEN

Step Five:
Confront Your Anger

In Patricia Evans's excellent book mentioned earlier, *The Verbally Abusive Relationship,* she notes that an addiction to anger grows out of the personal powerlessness of the abuser. Evans is sharing important insights we forget at our own peril. While we are probably not among the people who feel powerless in a way that could make us abusive, we do have the capacity to allow anger to turn into a daily routine. If crazymakers consistently make us feel inept, and we don't deal with our own anger, we may be setting ourselves up for a habit that *only hurts us.* Everyone must learn how to confront his or her anger.

It's important to remember that the driving tension behind the crazymaker operation is the need to stay in a position of control. After one of those terrible emotional explosions, the crazymaker leaves the encounter feeling good while the partner in the exchange feels bad. This is another reason we must come to grips with the animosity and wrath we naturally feel toward these people. Their drive to stay on top inevitably injures everyone around them and leaves us ruminating over the indignation left behind.

The question is *why* do we get so angry? Let's take a long look at the truth about anger and see what we conclude.

Facing the Facts

Anger is a normal human experience. The poet Maya Angelou once said, "I am capable of what every other human is capable of. This is one of the great lessons of war and life." Her logic leads us to conclude that every last one of us has a capacity for anger, and we will continually experience acrimony. Hidden behind our thoughts and memories may be the hope that we are different from the other irritated people of this world. Anger surely isn't part of our repertoire. It has to be a demonic intrusion slipped in when we were not looking. Really?

The great American psychiatrist Karl Menninger once noted that he didn't believe in the idea of a criminal mind. Instead, he had discovered that everyone has the capacity for criminal ideas. Interestingly enough, Albert Einstein agreed with him. No one is exempt from using the whole spectrum of emotion, ranging from loneliness to rage. While this conclusion may sound sinister, the truth is that anger has a highly significant place in everyone's life.

Even though most Christian people feel a bias against anger, it is an important part of our survival mechanism. The Scripture understands that it is inappropriate to ignore our negative feelings. After all, Jesus was angry when He drove the moneychangers out of the Temple (Luke 19:45–46). While it is a scandal to many contemporary theologians, the Old Testament is filled with references to the anger of God; of the 455 references to anger, 375 are about God's anger. Without anger we would be unable to register displeasure when we have been badly treated. In fact, anger mobilizes our emotional resources and prepares us to defend ourselves.

Changes the picture, doesn't it?

During the superficially tranquil period of the Victorian Era, anger was seen as a barbaric intrusion. While it was occasionally necessary for men, anger was strictly forbidden for women. Consequently, that rationale is still stuck between the edges of our own history, leaving behind the legacy that "good women" simply don't allow themselves a stroll down this path of expression. Because men are "more rational" than those "overly emotional" women, they can be trusted with angry feelings in a way that women simply can't handle. At least that was the old party line.

You buying this? We hope not. Research has indicated there is little difference between what men and women feel. Both experience anger and must learn how to deal with it. Whatever is wrong with you, it certainly has nothing to do with your periodically getting angry. Failure to face this fact can wreck your emotional life. Consider Helen.

Helen Sidwell showed up one Sunday in a church pastored by Dr. Robert Wise. She was so pressed against the wall that Robert almost walked past without seeing the woman. When he stopped to talk with her, Helen kept staring at the floor and appeared near tears. A decent conversation was not possible.

Several days later, Pastor Wise went by Helen's apartment to visit this new member of the community, only to discover she was so emotional it was once again nearly impossible to talk with her. Helen kept crying and didn't focus on his questions very well. Dr. Wise left with the impression that Helen was a single person, struggling with some trauma she hadn't resolved. Such was not the case!

Helen Sidwell had just gone through a horrendous divorce with an overbearing, tyrannical, abusive husband. Beaten down by his constant tirades and threats, with great reluctance and pain she had signed the supervision of their two children over to him, packed her car, and driven across three states, trying to escape any more assaults from this crazymaker. She had shown up in the church where Robert

Wise was pastor as more of an act of desperation than spiritual intention. She had no idea what to do with her life and felt completely worthless and broken. Most important, Helen was certain she was not angry.

Somewhere along the way, Helen had become convinced that God was so opposed to anger, He would punish those who let themselves fall victim to hostile feelings. What did she do with all of the venom, the hostility, the indignation, and wrath she felt toward her ex-husband? You got it. She stuffed, or repressed, the bad feelings. Her soured anger turned into the vinegar of depression, and more than occasionally she thought about suicide.

Robert's first task in guiding Helen toward a normal, positive condition was to assist her in getting in touch with what was buried in her soul. During this period, he helped Helen grasp the fact that she must stop running from her anger. God would not punish her for feeling righteous indignation against a husband who had beaten her into the ground. It was time to take a stand against the crazymaker who used her anger as one of his weapons!

Anger Is Not Bad?

A turning point for Helen came when she discovered a copy of Gary Oliver and H. Norman Wright's book *Good Women Get*

Angry. In the church's library, Helen stumbled across this guide to handling anger, depression, anxiety, and stress. Thumbing through the pages, she hit the chapter describing anger as the forbidden emotion. Helen knew instantly that she had found an important source of information on her problem. She quickly discovered a chapter listing eight misbeliefs about anger, recognizing her own error in the first of these.

Misbelief number one explored the commonly held idea that the Bible says anger is a sin. Surprisingly, the authors state, the Bible does *not* teach that anger is a sin. Rather, anger is recognized as legitimate and valid.

Helen was amazed. *Good Women Get Angry* explained that anger is a healthy, appropriate, and realistic emotion. The authors note that the *New American Standard* translation of the Scripture interprets Ephesians 4:26–27 more accurately than older versions: "BE ANGRY, AND yet DO NOT SIN; do not let the sun go down on your anger, and do not give the devil an opportunity."

Wright and Oliver clarified that the real issue was not in being angry, but in deciding *how to express the feeling*. That was the big question everyone must work through.

As Helen Sidwell read these words, she turned a significant corner in her thinking. For the first time, Helen knew it was not only right, but also important to express the anger she had felt when her husband put her in a compromising and unfair position.

Learning to Be Friends with Your Anger

Helen Sidwell slowly began to understand aspects of anger that she had not noticed before. Her anger was actually secondary to her primary feelings of hurt and fear. But anger had been her first warning sign that she was losing control of her life.

Anger warns us we don't want to walk through any more of the crazymaker's bed of nails. Regardless of what anyone else thinks about our situation, our values are being violated. Anger tells us that we are being pushed beyond our limits and capacities of response.

In this sense, anger is one of the ways God protects us. *Anger is, in fact, a God-given experience.* We have been given a divine emotional signal in our heads that tells us when we are getting too near the edge. Like semaphore lights at a dangerous train crossing, anger tells us to pay careful attention.

We often have a difficult time grasping the constructive use of anger. Our anger gets stirred up with hate, rage, aggression, losing control, and hostility, but these feelings are actually different from anger. Often these confusing emotions lead people to run from their anger, rather than learning how it can work for us.

Helen Sidwell had only been sure of one thing in her marriage: Anger was bad, and she'd better not get upset, or God would punish her. The result was that her anger had nowhere to go but inward. As Robert Wise worked with Helen, he taught her how to allow what was brewing inside to come out. First, she had to be clear that *anger is not hate*.

Hate surrounds itself with an ugliness that causes sensitive people to run. No one wants to live with the hostility engendered when they feel despised. However, hate is a very different experience from anger. While anger is an inner response to displeasure, pain, or being wounded, hate is the strong desire to loathe someone to the point of injuring him or her. You can be angry with anyone without having the slightest desire to hurt that person.

Helen Sidwell started realizing that she could be extremely angry with her ex-husband without hating him. Hate would only affect her in a negative way, but allowing herself to feel the anger his actions had engendered could become an important part of her healing process. Without having any intention of doing violence to her ex-husband, Helen began to think about the harsh treatment she had received at his hand. She was on her way to a new place.

Second, Helen needed to learn to think of anger as an alarm system that goes off when something is going wrong in our world. The tension we feel as our anger starts to build tells us that we are in a position of jeopardy. Ignoring the warning only creates deeper vulnerability to the approaching pain. On the other hand, if we allow anger to work, it has the capacity to galvanize us with the emotional armor we need for battle.

Third, Helen had to see how her anger could push her toward the higher ground she needed to find. She needed to gain new insight into her situation.

Rather than striking back, we must discover the thoughtful place where we want to stand. Anger often helps people decide that they have had enough harassment, and they will no longer leave themselves in a vulnerable position. While setting some boundaries may seem threatening at first, anger reminds us of how important it is to establish and maintain limits.

Steps Toward Change

Here are some steps that Dr. Wise suggested to Helen Sidwell as he helped her to turn anger into her friend. Perhaps, you can approach your own anger with a crazy-maker by using the following guidelines. These steps can brace you for change.

Step 1: Decide to experience your anger when it happens. Don't hide or ignore the feeling. Let the changes in your body—an increased heart rate, flushed skin, or the rise in your voice—relay their message. Make a firm decision that you will not run from anger in the future.

Step 2: Review what caused you to become angry. Analyze conversation and interaction with a crazymaker until you can isolate what you perceived as destructive. Pay careful attention to words and actions that "push your buttons."

Step 3: Make reflective notes on what causes you to be angry. Keeping a diary helps you stay in touch with the issues as you record conversations, actions, and your perceptions. Don't allow yourself to let these valuable insights slip away. Keep the diary in a confidential place, but close enough that you can make any reference needed to stay in touch with the problem.

Step 3 was the place where Helen made an important breakthrough. As she journaled about what had occurred in her struggles with her husband, Helen recognized the addictive pattern Patricia Evans warned about in *The Verbally Abusive Relationship*. Her husband was addicted to anger.

Ben Sidwell was a man without insight. He never examined his relationships with people and seemed to function without any awareness of how he hurt others. The man certainly had all the characteristics of a narcissist. Often changing jobs, he was also not a particularly effective person. Recognizing Ben's personal powerlessness helped Helen identify what had happened in many of their destructive encounters.

Helen realized that Ben was a man filled with many, many inner tensions. Like a water kettle spewing hot steam, Ben got rid of the suppressed hostility he carried by blasting

Helen. Tragically, Helen was the one left with the burns.

By charting on a piece of paper how their fights occurred, Helen began to recognize that a cycle existed. When Ben began having trouble at work, he easily became irritated with unimportant issues at home. The tension would build until finally Ben blew up, blaming everything on Helen who generally stood there with her mouth open, taking the shellacking as if she had it coming.

Helen could see that Ben was addicted to his anger as a means of release, an ineffectual way to handle the issues that he totally ignored. Once he attacked her, Ben was able to walk away feeling "like a man" because he had dominated his wife. After the explosion passed, Ben became much more gentle and pleasant. But then the tension started to build again, and the cycle started to repeat itself.

Rather than using his anger as God intended, Ben turned hostility into a crowbar with which to beat Helen. Now she had discovered why it was impossible to resolve their issues. Every aspect of Ben's behavior was actually an attempt to avoid facing his own limitations.

Step 4: Make decisions about how you will use your anger. Whether your anger moves you toward setting a boundary or reassessing a situation, this emotion is calling you to recognize some action you need to take. Helen Sidwell realized that she was not as worthless as she had thought. She rejected the depression she frequently felt and vowed never again to consider suicide. She also decided to get in touch with her children. She might have mistakenly signed them over to their narcissistic father, but she should still have visitation rights. She would discuss the matter with an attorney.

It is important to be clear about your intentions. Decide how to respond to your own anger in constructive ways. Write your intent for effective use of anger in the space below:

_____

_____

_____

Once a direction is established, your new decisions will allow anger to dissipate, since the emotion no longer has a reason for existence.

It is important for you to examine carefully how anger operates in your life. Look at it, examine it, write about it, and learn how to use it. That's the way you stop crazymakers from perpetuating harm.

Our fifth step out of chaos is to confront our anger.

chapter FIFTEEN

Step Six:
Allow Forgiveness to
Release the Pain

Crazymakers have a highly personal way of violating us, and because of this, the painful effect lasts and lasts! Unless we take appropriate action, the burning residual works in our nervous system years after a skirmish. We must learn how to clean out the residual effects of these explosions. And the best cleaning solution in the world is forgiveness!

Even though a crazymaker's behavior may have made us extremely angry, we still know it would be better to have this experience cleansed and our emotional security restored if possible. No matter how the other person has previously responded, we must attempt to forgive if we are going to approach the future effectively.

We believe the word *attempt* is well chosen because forgiveness can be extremely difficult, and it may take more time than we thought possible. In fact, we may have to make many attempts before we accomplish our goal, but it is worth the struggle.

Attempting a Hard Climb Up a High Mountain

A number of years ago, Dr. Robert Wise went through a difficult encounter that involved a number of people with an ample number of crazymakers among them. The matter ended in a collision of personalities that was devastating and without resolution, and a much larger circle of friends was hurt. Time went by and nothing was resolved.

Several years later Dr. Wise came to a personal turning point and wanted to attempt to gain closure on the old experience. No longer harboring ill will toward the people who had injured him, he wrote a letter to these individuals, hoping resolution would follow. It didn't happen. He did not receive letters, phone calls, or any form of personal contact that might have restored personal goodwill. The emptiness of the prolonged silence reminded him of how difficult attempts at forgiveness can be, but the effort was still important to him.

We believe that forgiveness is an important part of our personal development even if nothing else is accomplished. It's the way we keep the crazymaker's crazy from rubbing off!

Growing in the Darkness

The winner for the all-time collection of crazymakers situated in one place was Nazi Germany during the thirties and forties of the last century. How did a civilized nation with the highest level of scholarship and intellectual achievement fall into madness such as was generated by the Third Reich? The narcissism of Nazi racist radicals turned the state into a butchering machine that killed six million Jews and at least twenty million Russians. No one has ever fully calculated how many other people died across Europe and in the United States because of the Third Reich.

When World War II was over, plenty of forgiving was needed, and this hasn't stopped yet because many people are hanging on to their old animosities. While they have ample justification for ill will, these victims of World War II still carry grievances because they have been unable to forgive. Reviewing a few of these cases pushes us to recognize that no matter how difficult it may be, it is so much better to attempt to forgive.

Aya Ravid lived in Dresden, Germany, near the Czechoslovakian border with her family where Aya attended school not far from her home. By 1938, the violence against Jewish people had reached a frightening level, and her parents had begun to fear what might follow. Aya was smuggled out of the country with a group of Jewish girls and sent to what was then called Palestine to live on a kibbutz. Not until years later did Aya Ravid return to Dresden and discover that both of her parents had been shipped off to Auschwitz for execution. Aya had become a survivor of the Holocaust.

As the decades have gone by, Aya has struggled to live with her terrible memories. While it might be argued that the Nazis acted because of racism, the effect they had on Aya's life was similar to what happens when anyone is attacked by difficult and narcissistic people. Unfortunately, Aya was never able to find any means of forgiveness or a way to release the depth of her hostility. While she is now elderly, her pain is as real and harsh as it was decades ago.

In contrast, at almost the same time Aya left Germany, Corrie ten Boom was a prisoner in the Ravensbruck Concentration Camp because she hid Jewish people in her family home in Haarlem, Holland. Barely enduring the terrible persecution of the Nazis, Corrie survived the starvation and oppression of this Nazi hole of horror. Unfortunately her sister, Betsie, died in Ravensbruck.

After the war, Corrie was speaking in a church in Munich when she recognized in the congregation a man who had been one of the S.S. officers overseeing the Ravensbruck prison camp. When he came forward afterward to thank Corrie for her message proclaiming Jesus had died for all of our sins, she was confronted with a staggeringly painful decision. Could she personally forgive this man? Would she shake his hand? As Corrie allowed the love of Jesus to lead her, an extraordinary release followed, and she was able to forgive the man for what he had done to her and her sister Betsie. The past was settled.

Inability to forgive tells us one story; ability to pardon tells us another. We believe it is worth our effort to find a way out of the old hurts. Let's take a careful look at what forgiveness involves.

What Forgiveness Is Not

Over the years, we have found many people who struggle with forgiveness because they have misunderstood absolution. The following are some of the clarifications we often make during the counseling process.

Forgiveness is not forgetting that a bad experience ever

happened. Many times injured people believe they must rid themselves of memories of the past. This is not true. We don't forget old experiences because they are instructive and help us with the present moment.

Similarly, another conclusion people bring to the counseling office is that forgiving means condoning or approving what happened to them. This is also not true.

Forgiveness is not changing the rules on what is true, right, and appropriate. When people have lied, deceived, manipulated, or misconstrued, it is never acceptable, and we don't have to reshape the past to be able to forgive. *We neither forget nor reconstruct yesterday.* Forgiveness requires honesty that looks fully and completely at life as it is. We are not making an emotional decision so that hopefully we can go on our way once again as if everything is okay when we know it is not. Forgiveness must be honest.

Men often retreat from forgiving because they see it as a sign of weakness. They conclude that only ineffective people would stick their necks out, whereas a strong, virile man wouldn't make such a humbling gesture. Actually, dismissing a deed is an act of strength and courage. When we are convinced that—by any objective standard—we have been violated and yet make a decision to attempt to right the relationship, extraordinary capacity is required. Pardoning another person is an act of stamina and vigor that requires fortitude.

What Forgiveness Is

Forgiveness is recognizing that we are more than recipients of mistreatment, abuse, or injustice. While our feelings have been hurt, we are much more than the sum of these injuries, and we want our lives to go on without the weight of the old hurts. In order to climb above these barriers, we need to broaden our horizons.

Ever whack yourself on the thumb with a hammer? In a few seconds the size of the world is reduced to the same diameter as the head of the hammer. After the immediate ache has passed, our task is to remind ourselves that the world is still as big as it was before the accident.

We must make an honest decision that we want to move forward without our old hatreds and animosities. They serve no positive role in our lives, so therefore, we must be willing to lay them down—even though the decision may be difficult.

Forgiveness is a process that usually takes a considerable amount of time. We may decide to say a prayer of forgiveness, hoping that the issue is instantly finished, but it generally doesn't operate on a snap-decision basis. One of the reasons for delay is our own sense of pain. Often we will carry hurt that is physically painful so we cannot think about forgiveness until the pain subsides. We need to accept the fact that it will take time before we can reach the point where forgiveness is a genuine possibility.

Forgiveness is a reason for new self-esteem. Our self-worth rises as we practice releasing the grudges and hurts we have been carrying with us. We are actually recovering a power over ourselves that is a reason for personal worth. Anyone who has struggled to find release from hurt knows how difficult this path can be and that it takes a strong person to walk it.

The New Testament gives us strong wisdom: "You have heard that it was said, 'You shall love your neighbor, and hate your enemy.' But I say to you, love your enemies, bless those who curse you, do good to those who hate you, and pray for those who spitefully use you and persecute you, that you may be sons of your Father in heaven; for He makes His sun rise on the evil and on the good, and sends rain on the just and the unjust" (Matthew 5:43–45).

This passage reminds us that God deals with His world with a remarkable impartiality. When we are able to approximate the same, we have reached a high achievement.

Forgiveness is letting go of the negative feelings of the past. While we clearly remember what transpired, we will try to separate ourselves from the hurtful impact. The issue isn't whether anyone or everyone agrees with us or concurs in our decision. We are not going to struggle with destructive emotion any further.

As we have counseled hundreds of people over the years, we have found these clarifications helped many people break through the barriers that had kept them captive. Once the injured person is clear about what he or she is attempting to do, it is possible to take steps that lead to release.

Stages of Forgiveness

In the last chapter, we looked at Helen Sidwell's difficulty in confronting her own anger. We observed her slowly coming to the realization that she *had* been an angry person. You may have found yourself remembering your own anger as you read her story. If so, you may want to insert yourself and your difficult experience into each of these stages that lead to complete forgiveness.

Why not stop at this moment and review the interactive exercises you completed in the last chapter. How did the anger erupt, and why have you not been able to forgive this person? With your situation in hand, complete the following.

Step 1: Recognize who's responsible. Crazymakers often operate most destructively when they attack people with perfectionist tendencies. Having grown up worrying about doing everything right, we automatically assume that when something goes wrong it must be our fault. This tendency creates inappropriate responsibility, so we start blaming ourselves. Once we go down that road, we become even more of a perfectionist. The attack lowers our self-esteem, and we plow on as if it can be restored by working harder.

The first step toward forgiveness is recognizing that the responsibility wasn't ours in the first place. We need to let go of our self-blame. We may feel guilty, but it's not appropriate. Getting out from under carrying this overwhelming load will help us see the problem in a different light and put us in a position to start thinking about forgiveness.

How does the anger you have experienced fit this description? You may not have blamed yourself, but at least make a careful check so that you are not carrying more than your share of the load.

Step 2: Recognize any denial. Often the attack has been so painful that we would rather dismiss the memory. "Let's just not talk about it," was the favorite retort of a woman who dealt with the past by simply denying it. A sensitive woman, Evelyn cried easily and was always uncomfortable weeping in front of other people. Her approach to a difficult situation was simply to change the subject. Yet her denying her own emotions only deepened the hole she lived in.

Denial can take many forms. While we tend to think of it as the refusal to recognize a fact, it is also the attempt *to avoid thinking* about something that we know is true. In the movie *Gone With the Wind,* Scarlett O'Hara's answer to seemingly impossible worries was, "I'll think about it tomorrow." Sometimes we postpone forgiveness, hoping another day will bring some change in a situation buried in us.

Similar to denial, many people cling to a victim mentality, settling into a pool of remorse and regret. Charles Dickens paints a frightening picture of how toxic the victim mentality can be in *Great Expectations*. Miss Haversham was left at the altar only to return home a bitter, angry woman. In her crumbling mansion, she still wore her rotting wedding dress to remind her of her pain. Finally Miss Haversham found a ward with an inclination to break men's hearts. The toxic poison of Haversham's inability to forgive spilled over into the child's life, contaminating her as well.

Take another look at the effect a crazymaker has had in your life. Has it been difficult to be honest about resolving this issue? Have you allowed the pain to linger far too long? Is it possible you let yourself slip into a victim role? In Everett Worthington's *Five Steps to Forgiveness*, he uses the phrase "detoxifying our soul" to describe the importance of ridding ourselves of ill will that can only be cleansed by forgiveness.

The time has come to detoxify your emotions. Take a long, hard look and allow yourself to be totally honest about your past and present feelings.

Step 3: Recover the value of suffering. At the time we were injured, we saw no value in the experience. One of the important insights the Christian faith imparts is the redemptive value hidden in undeserved suffering. If we are struggling to forgive, recovering this aspect of a past affliction can help us press on.

Step 4: Pursue recovery. Recovery sometimes begins as we start to pray for the crazymaker. Jesus instructed us to do this. While we may pray a long time before we see any hint of change, prayer still opens the doors that are locked with keys that no longer exist. If nothing else, prayer has an effect in our hearts.

Praying sets the stage for a possible next step. We may want to attempt to sit down with the person who hurt us. The hope would be to say with sincerity, "I forgive you." We certainly don't want to use that sentence as another means of revenge. Even though the crazymaker may be resistant to change and healing, the goal is to let him or her know that we will no longer resist being restored to a new relationship. While we recognize that many crazymakers will ignore responsibility, speaking the words of forgiveness can facilitate reconciliation in our hearts.

No one can predict the crazymaker's response. In fact, he or she may become hostile and defensive. If so, we have no other choice but to go on our way, knowing we did the best we could. While we are not forgiving simply to make ourselves feel better, the truth is that forgiveness sets in motion a chain response that is part of the method God uses to heal the world. On the other hand, anger and hostility turn the process around and send viciousness across the globe. We believe that anyone is far better off to stand on the side of God's plan than to live in his or her own brokenness.

Have you made a decision to forgive, regardless of how the other party receives your actions? At some moment, you must cross the line and make a firm commitment to stand in a new place. You cannot be pushed into such a decision until you are ready for it. However, you have to make a decision. Is now the right time? Think about it before you go on. This could be the time to cross the line. Sometimes we hang on to our anger because we want to wait until we see vengeance on our abuser, but we must turn vengeance over to God. He promises to take care of it eventually.

Renewal

Almost everything Jesus tells us to do also has a hidden value that is discovered only as we live out His teaching. No matter how difficult and broken our life has been, forgiveness has the power to give back our worth and value as a human being. Receiving that renewing grace is worth whatever it takes.

In Part 2 we have looked at six steps. Let's review those steps now.

GETTING THE "CRAZY" OUT

SIX STEPS OUT OF YOUR CRISIS

- Step 1: Identify the History of the Problem

- Step 2: Set Boundaries That Bring Change

- Step 3: Encourage Counseling

- Step 4: Find Friends to Support You in the Battle

- Step 5: Confront Your Anger

- Step 6: Allow Forgiveness to Release the Pain

part THREE

BEYOND CRAZY:

THE GIFT OF

SPIRITUAL

ENDURANCE

chapter SIXTEEN

Turning Suffering into Significance

A young father took his five-year-old son, Jason, out on the front porch. Putting the boy on the edge of the four-foot-high porch, Dad stood on the ground and told the child to jump. The child looked over the edge at what appeared to be a chasm and shook his head.

"Come on, Jason," the father said. "I'll catch you."

The son again shook his head.

"Hey! Don't you trust me?"

This time Jason hesitated a moment and then nodded yes.

"Good. Now jump."

Catching a big breath, Jason leaped toward his father's

arms. Dad abruptly jumped back and let the child crash to the ground.

With tears running down his face, Jason looked up and whimpered. "What happened?"

"Let that be a lesson to you, son. Don't ever trust anyone again!"

Such a story takes our breath away. We can feel the bewildered child staggering back into the house with his heart broken. Our imaginations lead us down the road into the future, wondering what will become emotionally of such an injured child. The truth is this is a parable about narcissists and their victims. Both sides of these struggles can end up damaged like five-year-old Jason. The world becomes a place filled with enemies, and we need help in turning our suffering into significance.

Turning the World Right Side Up

We are living in a time of fear. At every level, Americans fear foreigners, immigrants, and travelers as possible terrorists and spies. The sounds of conflict roll across the planet from Iraq to Korea to Israel, and on to the hole in the ground that was once the World Trade Center in New York City. People talk about the Tim McVeighs and Terry Nicholses of the world as they once remembered baseball players. The result is that fear keeps on spreading, with the crazymakers apparently winning.

Finding an answer is extremely important if we are going to live in personal peace. Struggles with difficult people can leave us afraid and apprehensive, needing to find a remedy to push worry aside. In addition to what we have written in the previous chapters, we believe there is another answer for anyone struggling to find tranquillity.

In the apostle John's first letter he wrote, "There is no fear in love; but perfect love casts out fear . . . We love, because He [God] first loved us" (1 John 4:18–19 NASB). The apostle is saying that only love can liberate us from the bondage created by mistrust and anxiety. The followers of Jesus saw in His actions (and learned by following His teaching) that love has an extraordinary power to unlock the chains that bind people. A loving person might be small or physically weak, but love gives this person the capacity to overcome barriers of any size. Love can turn the world right side up.

LOVE IS YOUR ANSWER

Having read the foregoing chapters, you know love is not a spineless submission to the pressure of difficult people. Sometimes love must take the form of setting boundaries, maintaining discipline, and insisting on correct behavior. When our ultimate goal is love, we may be able to help our crazymakers as well as ourselves.

LOVE STOPS PROJECTION

Several years ago, a minister/counselor was working with a number of heroin addicts. He quickly saw the need for a methadone clinic that would help addicts get off heroin usage. The plan seemed simple enough and would help the entire community. With a significant donor offering financial assistance, he set out to explore the idea of starting a clinic with services to be provided *in another part of the city*, far away from his church.

Boom!

Word spread like wildfire from unnamed sources that the good reverend was hauling in addicts, thieves, murderers, and liars from every corner of the earth to burglarize the neighborhood where his church was located, as well as attack the children. He was going to use a church like a crack house! Radio talk shows broadcasted the screams of citizens. Television stations and newspapers carried the story of an irate public. Finally, the pastor held a public meeting in the church to dispel the rumors. After announcing the misinformation and conveying the truth, the meeting still lasted for two and a half explosive hours!

What would the minister have gotten out of this clinic? Not one dime! He was only trying to help terribly needy people, but that didn't stop the destructive responses. Attempting to do loving things doesn't always have a happy ending . . . but it can still set us free from fear!

During America's Great Depression, the newly elected president made one of the most important speeches in the nation's history. With crushing financial problems squeezing the life out of the country, Franklin D. Roosevelt proclaimed, "The only thing we have to fear is fear itself." He wanted to break the strangling clutch that apprehension had on the public. Millions of people were standing around hungry, pointing fingers, and this only made matters worse. The problem? *Projection!*

Why did that minister become the target of good people who overnight turned into screaming vigilantes? *Projection.* They saw him as the target for the fears they didn't know how to deal with, and the battle was on. In a similar way, narcissistic people can rattle us, creating panic, and suddenly our fears are being projected onto other people. It happens every day.

Love changes the equation by insisting we see the other individual as a person, rather than a thing. No matter how disruptive a narcissist is, he or she is still a human being and a child of God. We can insist on responsible behavior without turning crazymakers into icons of unmitigated malice and deceit.

LOVE STOPS GUILT

As we observed earlier when people have been attacked, they may think it was their fault. In addition to the humiliation of the attack, they feel guilty for having been the target!

Sound strange? Not if you've spent hours worrying over, "What *did I do* to cause this problem?" At such times, we need the cleansing power of love to set us free.

When Scripture tells us, "we love, because He first loved us," we are reminded that God's love was first extended to us when we were guilty people. His forgiveness set us free from the accusations of our own consciences. In the same way, divine forgiveness releases us from the phony guilt that weighs us down.

Get back in touch with the caring, forgiving, restorative side of love. Allow the warmth of a kind, caring God to unhook the locks that guilt uses to keep negative experiences in your mind. Love will set you free of the accusations!

LOVE OFFERS SIGNIFICANCE

During World War II, Victor Frankl was a Viennese psychiatrist imprisoned by the Germans only because he was Jewish. Faced with staggering suffering and terrible torture in Auschwitz, Frankl did not expect to survive. However, as he worked on the meaningless jobs the Nazis gave him to perform in freezing weather, Frankl made a surprising discovery: he had the mental ability to attribute meaning and purpose to his horrible surroundings. Frankl could remember people he loved and cared about. Getting back in touch with precious memories transformed the present moment. No longer was Frankl a slave, a cog in an evil machine. Love reminded him that he was a human being. Victor Frankl survived through the power of love because in the midst of his suffering, love elevated him to a new level of humanity.

The possibility of surrounding our suffering with love puts us at the threshold of a door to a new world. We may not be able to change the crazymakers in our life any more than Frankl could transform the Nazis, but we still have the capacity to give any situation new meaning and purpose. In so doing, love can take us to a fresh place of new possibility.

No matter how painful our emotional injury has been, we will not allow animosity to linger inside us as a permanent resident. Only the best thoughts and intentions will govern our lives. We decide to maintain that level of meaning regardless of what has happened or will happen. This is how love can set anyone free.

Remember Jason?

Jason's father had stuck a painful message into his five-year-old son's mind: *Don't trust anybody!* With time, Jason came to see that idea was not true. Certainly plenty of people in the world were not reliable, but good people were also standing on every street corner. Jason had to reexamine the experience that distrust had burned in his mind. He could not let a difficult father undermine the entire direction of his life.

As Jason wrestled with his negative feelings, he came to an important insight. He had two fathers! Certainly his earthly father was a difficult man, but Jason's heavenly Father was a gracious, loving parent who had first loved him before Jason even recognized God's existence. Jason needed to allow the love of God to be the new reconstructive force in his life. Jason's decision to trust God's love was the start of healing his past experiences.

Why not pause now and make a decision to allow love to be the last word in your life? No matter how badly a crazymaker may have injured you, your final thoughts and actions about this person will be recast. One of the things that the cross of Jesus teaches us is that some defeats can be more significant than victories. You will have your "Good Fridays," but they will lead you to Easter mornings!

chapterSEVENTEEN

The Transformation of Experience

From the first page forward, our goal has been to learn to live with . . .

> insensitive, tactless, careless, inattentive, difficult,
> self-absorbed, neglectful, damaging, condemning,
> harsh, hard, treacherous, deceiving, prejudiced,
> and paralyzing people.

Have you made it yet?
Don't give up. You can!
You can transform your experience into a blessing.

Transformation? You're Kidding!

The previous chapters have chronicled the struggles of people like Jack Smith and Sally Harris to deal emotionally with the indifference of their spouses. We have considered the pain of Amy Littleton and Helen Sidwell as well as others confronted by difficult people. Some were able to change their situations; some were not. Regardless of the outcome, it is usually a painful journey. We want to take a final look at the possibilities for a transformation of our hurtful experiences, because Christians have a promise of more than recovery.

The apostle Paul wrote, "For I consider that the sufferings of this present time are not worthy to be compared with the glory that is to be revealed to us"(Romans 8:18 NASB). Since Paul didn't clarify what he meant by suffering, we can conclude that the promise runs the gamut from martyrdom to clashes with narcissistic people. The promise of Scripture was that through our struggles a glorious change could be revealed *in us*.

Such a promise may be hard to believe. Counselors are far more likely to hear strugglers complain about their heartaches. In fact, a counselor is most apt to hear, "Why did this happen to me?" Actually, this question cannot be answered in a way that is emotionally satisfying for the sufferer.

For change to begin, we need to ask a different question. *What can I do with this struggle? How can I take what has happened and remold the brokenness into a new shape with new promise?* Once we start to answer that query, the sun begins to arise on our dark night.

The apostle Paul wrote a powerful and specific passage on this issue:

> Blessed be the God and Father of our Lord Jesus Christ, the Father of mercies and God of all comfort; who comforts us in all our affliction so that we may be able to comfort those who are in any affliction with the comfort with which we ourselves are comforted by God. (2 Cor. 1:3–4 NASB)

When we make it our goal to pass hope and consolation on to other people, we have started to emerge from the hole a crazymaker put us in. God can help you, and you can help others.

Dr. Meier and Dr. Wise have found three important insights that have helped hundreds of people find the spiritual endurance they needed to live beyond "crazy."

The Road to Change

The first step is to remember that our struggles are shared by Jesus. When a crazymaker is rocking our world and turning it upside down, we feel extremely alone and broken. However, feelings of loneliness are incorrect. Far from being abandoned, Jesus is standing at our side. Knowing that He is with us imparts courage.

Logic suggests that if we have a child lingering at the edge of death, then God must surely be with us. However, if we are attempting to get over the stinging words of a crazymaker, the problem isn't as significant and He probably isn't paying attention to us. Right? Wrong!

God is as concerned with the least of our struggles as He is with the weightiest of them. Don't ever withdraw because you don't feel your need is worthy enough. *Pain is pain regardless of how it comes to us.*

Jesus still stands with us in the least of our struggles.

Isaiah said, "When you pass through the waters, I will be with you; And through the rivers, they will not overflow you. When you walk through the fire, you will not be scorched, Nor will the flame burn you" (Isaiah 43:2 NASB). The prophet didn't say "if," but "when." The Scripture fully expects everyone to face floods and fires, *but not to walk through them alone.*

The second step toward transformation is to remember that our struggles are meant to teach us important lessons. While crazymakers can drive us to total distraction, they also may accidentally impart wisdom far greater than *they have the ability* to recognize.

C. S. Lewis once wrote that suffering is God's megaphone. He said that God whispers to us in our pleasures, speaks to us in our consciences, but shouts at us in our pain. The Scriptures tell us again and again that personal struggle clarifies which individuals God finds acceptable for leadership in His future plans. The stories of Joseph, David, Gideon, Jeremiah, and many more heroes of faith depict undeserved cruelty and injustice, but in the end these people of faith rise to the top through what they learned in the hard times. The pain in Moses' life prepared him to face down the Pharaoh of Egypt decades later. *He learned from what he endured.*

There is nothing romantic about our struggles and suffering; they are always hard. Yet the moments when we feel most overwhelmed often become times when we experience the power of God's unexpected impartations of grace most dramatically. On some far-off distant morning, we wake up and realize God used the past to give us a crucial perspective for today's problems.

One of the highest moments in the story of Christian redemption occurred the day before Jesus died on the cross as He knelt in the Garden of Gethsemane praying, "My Father, if it is possible, let this cup pass from Me: yet not as I will, but as Thou wilt" (Matthew 26:39 NASB). In the agony of that prayer, Jesus declared He would fully agree to accept pain in order that every purpose of God could be accomplished. The result changed the course of human history—then, now, and forever.

Accept the fact that even the nonsense of crazymakers can be used by God to teach you something you need to know. Maybe undeserved circumstances will prepare you for yet-unseen service. Transformation starts with the decision to learn from your undeserved past conflicts.

The third step is to affirm that our difficulties are meant to be transformed. We may not see the result in six months, a year, or even a decade, but we have made a decision to stand on this promise, regardless of where it takes us. We lift our eyes above the skirmish at hand and insist that every pain will be remembered in the light of eternity.

Time is an amazing revealer of God's finest desires and intentions. The passing of the days clarifies the truth in ways we often would never have expected. St. Francis of Assisi offered us an example of transformation. Living in a time of fear, ignorance, and misunderstanding, Francis believed he was called of God to build up the church. He first assumed this meant reconstructing buildings, but with time he came to see the purpose was much, much larger than he ever envisioned. Francis had been called to be a transformer of the faith of the people.

In his famous prayer to be made into an instrument of peace, St. Francis prayed that his life would be filled with transforming purpose. Where there was hate, he prayed to sow love. If there was injury, Francis wanted to leave pardon. People of doubt would discover faith. Actually, Francis of Assisi was praying *to be the agent of transformation.*

Rather than only seeking change for himself, Francis lived a lifetime goal of being the bearer of change. When some important ingredient was missing, this humble man of God prayed for the ability to carry that needed element into the disturbed situation. You have the same capacity.

Crazymakers tend to make us think about revenge, retribution, and retaliation. We can even become obsessed with self-justification. St. Francis sets us on a different path, calling us to accomplish self-effacement. The mere act of considering such a path is the start of transformation. Much to our surprise, the call of God is for us also to become a transformer of the faith of others. Such a possibility is living far, far beyond crazy in the land where your experiences can be redeemed.

A Concluding Thought

Is there one last word we might leave with you as you return to the task of living with crazymakers? Perhaps the apostle Paul stated it as completely as it could be said:

> Therefore we also, since we are surrounded by so great
> a cloud of witnesses, let us lay aside every weight, and

the sin which so easily ensnares us, and let us run with endurance the race that is set before us, looking unto Jesus, the author and finisher of our faith, who for the joy that was set before Him endured the cross, despising the shame, and has sat down at the right hand of the throne of God. For consider Him who endured such hostility from sinners against Himself, lest you become weary and discouraged in your souls. (Hebrews 12:1–3)

The healing power of God will turn our losses into victories. Remembering this fact will help keep us from growing weary and losing heart. He is our answer to spiritual endurance. *Jesus is the transformer of our experience.*

His goal for us is to become a . . .
disciplined, boundary-setting, understanding but firm,
insightful, consistent, enduring, realistic,
stable, self-evaluating, reflective,
supportive, forgiving, forgiven,
balanced, loving, and protected person.

About the Authors

Nationally recognized psychiatrist and founder of the Meier Clinics (1-888-7-CLINIC), **Paul Meier, M.D.,** is cohost of the national radio show *Meier Clinic Program*. He is also the best-selling author or coauthor of more than seventy books, including *Love Is a Choice, Happiness Is a Choice, Don't Let Jerks Get the Best of You, Mood Swings,* and *Love Hunger.* Meier also collaborated on the best-selling Millennium series, which includes three futuristic novels. He holds an M.D. degree from the University of Arkansas College of Medicine and completed his psychiatric residency at Duke University. To find out more about the Meier Clinics and Dr. Meier, go to www.meierclinics.com.

Author of twenty-seven published books, **Robert L. Wise, Ph.D.,** also writes for numerous magazines and journals, including *Christianity Today, Leadership*, and *The Christian Herald*. He is a bishop in the communion of Evangelical Episcopal Churches. He collaborated on the national best-selling Millennium series, which includes *The Third Millennium, The Fourth Millennium,* and *Beyond the Millennium,* and is the author of *Be Not Afraid* and *Spiritual Abundance*. In addition, he recently released the Sam & Vera Sloan Mystery Series, including *The Empty Coffin, The Dead Detective*, and *Deleted*.

LOVE IS A CHOICE:
THE DEFINITIVE BOOK ON LETTING GO OF UNHEALTHY RELATIONSHIPS

DR. ROBERT HEMFELT
DR. FRANK MINIRTH
DR. PAUL MEIER

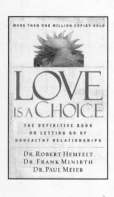

This number-one national best-seller and groundbreaking book on recovery for codependent relationships is newly repackaged.

These best-selling doctors walk you through their ten proven stages to recovery from codependency that results from external circumstances. Humans are susceptible to codependency because of our sinful tendency to use defense mechanisms to fool ourselves. In codependent relationships, deceitful games are played, and important Christian principles are often taken out of context and abused. God wants us to have healthy relationships with a balance between being dependent and independent. The doctors describe how the most effective means of overcoming codependent relationships is to establish or deepen a relationship with Christ Himself. They describe the causes of codependency, pointing out the factors that perpetuate it, and lead readers through their ten stages of recovery.

ISBN: 0-7852-6375-6